DOUBLE GRACE

55 Thoughts on Our Identity in Christ
By Caleb Gibson

Unless otherwise noted, all Scripture is taken from the New American Standard Bible.

ISBN 978-0-578-36076-8

Printed by KDP

DEDICATION

To my Grandparents, Reuben (Pawpaw), and Ramona (Mimi) Meadors. Pawpaw, even though you are not here to read this, I am thankful God placed me in my life. You were a WWII veteran, and it's because of people like you who had the bravery to serve in our military that I was able to write this book in freedom. To me when I picture Heaven, I see us sitting across a circle table. Me and you are talking about the 2017 Astros Championship season while playing a game of dominoes.

Mimi, you see the best in everyone. When Paul wrote to the young Pastor Timothy he once said, "For I am mindful of the sincere faith within you, which first dwelt in your grandmother Lois and your mother Eunice, and I am sure that *it is* in you as well." (2 Timothy 1:5). Mimi, thank you for being my Lois. You really represent God's unconditional love. You would give the coat off your back, the food one your plate, and your last piece of your favorite, Doublemint gum.

CONTENTS

ENDORSEMENTS

This book is like a box of Cadbury's favorites! A variety of yummy bite size chocolates all together in one pack. Within this book are all the delicious morsels of grace. Caleb captures the essence of all the truths of grace and presents them in their simplicity and beauty. This book isn't complex and verbous, it's efficient and potent. You don't have to read it from start to finish. You can pick it up anytime and turn to any chapter and be absolutely blessed. This book is perfect for new believers and anyone who wants to discover the glory of the grace of God. It's ideal for a daily devotion, for short Bible studies, for quick reads or for anyone wanting to delve deeper into grace. I highly recommend Double Grace by Caleb Gibson. As a box of Cadbury 's favourites would bring joy to your body so Double Grace will bring joy to your soul!

– **Ryan Rufus**, www.NewNatureMinistries.org

Pastor Caleb is not only someone I know personally but is also someone whose life radiates the grace of God. I know that is also something you will encounter as you read this book. Every day, as you pick it up you will receive a fresh encounter of God's grace and love for you. I also believe this book will stir your faith and remind you that if God is for you who can be against you.

- **Pastor Larry Martinez**, New Covenant Church of El Campo, Texas

www.NewCovenantWay.com

"Caleb is a wonderful and genuine man of God that brings the message of grace to the table in a simple, yet powerful way. Many Christians know about the amazing grace of God, but not many know it to the point that they truly understand who they are in Christ. With this book, you'll learn who you are in God's eyes. In the end, what He says about you is all that really matters. Take a leap of faith and finally discover the truth of your identity in God."

- **Pastor Jamey Escamilla**, New Covenant Church of El Campo, Texas

"Whether you are new in your faith or a seasoned Christian, Pastor Caleb Gibson's book will help you discover on a deeper level who you are, as you discover who Christ is. Pastor Caleb unpacks 55 "you are" statements that will cause you to grow in your knowledge of Jesus. If you desire to understand God's multiplied grace to you then this book is for you."

- **Pastor Noe Cano,** Harvest Time Church in Bay City Texas

"Caleb Gibson's work in 'Double Grace' is truly a manifestation of what God's grace can produce in a person's life. Pastor Caleb writes from a place of personal revelation and interaction with the truths contained within this book. 'Double Grace' is destined to minister the same grace that its author has experienced into the lives of all who read it with an open heart. I continue to enjoy the blessing I have received from reading 'Double Grace'.

- **Pastor Chris Barhorst,** True Life Church Greenville, Ohio
Author of "The Redemptive Book of Revelation"

"It is my honor to heartily recommend "Double Grace" by my friend Pastor Caleb Gibson. This book is saturated with Good News. So saturated, in fact, that your head may attempt to protest. But, if it does, don't fret. Just listen to your heart instead and allow God to saturate you with the incredibly Good News of His marvelous grace! The thoroughly biblical content of this book will no doubt edify, encourage, and empower you. And it may very well change your relationship with God and life as a whole. Prepare to be saturated in "double-grace"!

- **Pastor Jordan Orick,** The Glory Center in Portage, Michigan

"Caleb paints a powerful picture of our true identity in Christ. His extraordinary ability to apply scripture to clearly illustrate who Jesus is and who we are in Him, helps build a strong and solid foundation for us to stand on. He persistently points us to all that we have in Christ: hope, love, strength, purpose, power and so much more! Double Grace will bring blessing and encouragement to your journey with God. Simply put, his words will stir and warm your heart. May we all live and walk in multiplied grace!"

- **Associate Pastor Bobby Williams,** IGNITE Church in Bay City, Tx

FOREWORD

I have a confession to make. I'm a recovering legalist. One might not expect that from me, a "grace preacher", but it's true. While I grew up in an amazing Christian home, somewhere along the way I adopted a performance mindset regarding my relationship with the Lord. As long as I was living right, avoiding the many temptations of male adolescence, and attending the youth group at my church - I enjoyed the love of God. All it would take though is a single misstep. Nothing dramatic required. A simple improper thought would even be enough to send me into a tailspin of spiritual agony, doubting my salvation and questioning God's heart for me. According to my performance mindset, the only remedy of course was a session of intense 'Christian calisthenics', complete with Bible study, prayer, and if the sin was bad enough, fasting, sometimes for days at a time.

The irony was, that from a humanistic perspective, I was living an exceptionally moral life compared to most of my peers around me. I didn't drink, smoke, or do drugs, nor had I had pre-marital sex. These accomplishments, while good in and of themselves, were twisted in my head to formulate a spiritual ego that seemed to embrace the idea, at least on my good days, that, "God was pretty lucky to have me on his team." Obviously, I never said this out loud, but the internal seed of arrogance was there, that is, until I fell short in some way, triggering a manic and lingering sense of failure due to 'disappointing God'.

It wasn't that God didn't use me during this time, because he certainly did. I was regularly leading others to Christ and serving in various capacities in my church, but underneath it all, my pharisaical thinking prevented me from deriving lasting joy in my service to the Lord. Even if momentary joy was located, it didn't remain, because it was always met with uncertainty about my spiritual status. Looking back it was a very egotistical way to live, always focused on self. Without knowing it, I was elevating my performance over Jesus' work on the Cross. It would take me years to find freedom from the imprisonment I had found myself in due to a works-based theology.

When it finally would come, my personal liberation was found in Paul's letter to the Romans. Specifically, in the first and second chapter, I received a revelation for the first time in my life that apart from Christ, I was utterly depraved. You wouldn't think that this would help in the emotional rollercoaster of guilt that I was experiencing, but it did. For once and for all, I knew that righteousness could not be found in my performance, whether good or bad. I was leveled. Once this sunk in, for the first time in my life, I was dependent upon grace. For the first time, the comfort of a humble gratitude welled up in my heart.

Over the years my understanding and appreciation of God's grace has grown and matured, but that initial seed, straight from the scriptures, has never left me. Only since God showed me this in His Word have I found peace with Him. My life is still far from perfect, but I've become rooted in the fact that Christ took my place, trading my sin and shame, for His righteousness - a righteousness that is "by grace through faith", rather than works or spiritual performance.

Looking back, I can only imagine what a difference a book like this would have made in my life. How many years could it have prevented me from experiencing the trepidation and fear (as a Christian) of being judged by God. This revelation, I believe, has propelled Caleb's wisdom and spiritual insight well beyond his years. As a pastor, he is grounded, well-versed, and compassionate. I believe those traits emerge from the pages of this book and will bless all who peruse its pages. As humans, grace isn't always intuitive. In fact, it's quite contradictory to our nature, but this is exactly why it's so important that we allow the salve of God's grace and goodness to minister to us and redeem the scars that our time in Eden left behind.

Grace teaches,

Lucas Miles
Pastor & Author of Good God and The Christian Left
LucasMiles.org

PREFACE

How can grace be multiplied? The Apostle Paul once said, "Grace and peace be multiplied to you in the knowledge of God and of Jesus our Lord." (2 Peter 1:2). Grace is multiplied through the knowledge of Jesus.

In this world, we are all faced with a simple question, "Who am I?" **Our identity fundamentally changes how we value ourselves.** Your worth is not in your fame, or the car you drive, or how much you make an hour. It is found in Jesus Christ. These things are important but they should not be the sole identity of our life. It's time to see ourselves the way God does.

In the Bible, the number 5 represents grace. This book contains 55 lessons about your identity in Christ. My goal in writing this book is to point you towards the Gospel. This a book written to believers in Christ. You can read a chapter a day. As you go throughout your day meditate on what Christ has done for us on the cross. It is about knowing Christ personally. This book is a personal discovery of your new identity in Christ.

Blaise Pascale, a Christian Philosopher in the 1600s once said, "Not only do we know God by Jesus Christ alone, but we know ourselves only by Jesus Christ." **The more we know Jesus, the more we know our true identity.** The majority of these chapters show us a picture of who God is. This is not only a study on who we are, it is also a study on who God is. God is holy, worthy, and righteous.

The grace and love of Christ surpasses our knowledge. The Apostle Paul once told the Church in Ephesus, "so that Christ may dwell in your hearts through faith. And I pray that you, being rooted and established in love, may have power, together with all the Lord's holy people, to grasp how wide and long and high and deep is the love of Christ, and to know this love that **surpasses knowledge**—that you

 may be filled to the measure of all the fullness of God." (Ephesians 3:17-19). A standard measuring tape is incapable of measuring God's great grace! In fact there is really no way through our knowledge to understand how much God loves us. God's unmerited favor is unending.

How do we get double grace, triple grace, or a multiplication of grace? We receive it through the knowledge of Jesus! When you wake up and are aware of God's presence there is more grace. I think everyone knows that they've been given grace, but we do not fully understand the magnitude of it. Not only are you loved, you are more than loved. Not only are you forgiven, you are more than forgiven, righteous, significant, complete, and so much more!

(1) YOU ARE SO LOVED

Before the sun was out, the disciples crossed the sea in a boat. Suddenly they encounter a storm and see a man walking across the water. Their mind races to figure out what is going on. One disciple says, "It's a ghost," and they eventually realize who it is. It's their friend, their leader, it's Jesus! Peter then gets out of the boat and begins to walk on the water towards Jesus. The Bible says, **"But seeing the wind,** he became frightened, and beginning to sink, he cried out, 'Lord, save me!'"** (Matthew 14:30). Notice this verse begins by telling us what Peter saw, the winds. He began to sink when he took his eyes off of the Lord. Now it is impossible to walk on water during a storm. In fact it is still impossible to walk on water during a clear blue day. Here it was not about the waves, but it was about how Peter took his focus off Christ. This is what happens to us as believers when we take our focus and place it on something other than Christ.

Some Christians try to muster enough strength to love God. They try and try to love God but it always feels like it is not enough. My friend the Bible says, "We love, because He first loved us." (1 John 4:19). It is the very fact that we are conscious of this love that we will love God. God is the initiator. Now we love Him because He took the first step. The way to love God more is to understand and focus on how much God loves you.

Like Peter when we become worried with too many things, we can miss the moments God has for us. We can see all of the storms and waves and become distracted. Some people place an emphasis on our love for the Lord. This important and we should love God, but remember the main focus should be on God's love for us. The idea is not to ignore the storm and never bring an umbrella. We should be aware of the storm, but not allow it to control our lives. In these moments where we are conscious of God's love for us, we will love God more. Knowing God's love isn't a temporary motivation, it's a life-sustaining foundation. Remember, "We love, because He first loved us." (1 John 4:19).

> **Knowing God loves you isn't a temporary motivation, it's a life sustaining foundation.**

(2) YOU ARE RIGHTEOUS

Have you ever read a word in the Bible and never quite understood the meaning? I believe that this is how some view the word, righteousness. We know that it has meaning, but are we sure what that meaning is?

So what does righteousness mean? It means that we are right with God. E. W. Kenyon once said, "Righteousness means the ability to stand in the presence of the Father God without the sense of guilt or inferiority." This shows how Jesus stood in the presence of God. He wasn't afraid, He was speaking with His father.

So what do we do to get righteousness? We freely receive it as a gift. The Bible says, "For if by the transgression of the one, death reigned through the one, much more those who receive the abundance of grace and of the gift of righteousness will reign in life through the One, Jesus Christ" (Romans 5:19). This verse says that we need two things, an abundance of grace and the gift of righteousness. Notice how righteousness is described as a gift instead of something you earn. There is no way to be righteous by our own efforts. It is by the obedience of Christ. We receive it by faith. When we realize this, it will change our walk with God. No longer should we try to earn our place with God.

The Bible explains that, "He made Him who knew no sin to be sin on our behalf, so that we might become the righteousness of God in Him." (2 Corinthians 5:21). On the cross Jesus made a beautiful exchange. **He swapped our sin with His righteousness.** Now we can understand the value of this word. Now we can always have a relationship with God. This is one of the greatest gifts. Righteousness is not just another word that we use; it represents one of the main purposes of the Cross.

(3) YOU ARE UNDER GRACE

"And the Child grew and became strong in spirit, filled with wisdom; and the grace of God was upon Him." (Luke 2:40). I love this verse because it explains how the grace of God was upon Jesus. He grew, became strong, and was full of grace. Now the Bible also tells us that where sin abounds, grace abounds all the more (Romans 5:20). Since we know that Jesus never sinned, how did He abound in grace? There must be another way to receive more grace.

If you want to have a fun Bible study, go throughout your Bible and notice the first mention of a word. The first time the Bible mentions the word, "grace" it is about Noah. This verse says, "But Noah found grace in the eyes of the LORD." (Genesis 6:8 NKJV). According to Strong's Concordance Noah's name means, "rest." In essence, the Hebrew translation of this verse explains that **rest found grace!**

Wow, this gives us insight into the life of Christ. Jesus was restful and, "the grace of God was upon Him." The more we rest and trust God, the more grace abounds in our life. Remember that Christ only duplicates what He see the Father doing, Jesus once said, "The Son can do nothing of Himself. He can do only what He sees

His Father doing" (John 5:19). This means that this is the attitude of God. Christ personified what it meant to live a life at rest.

It was the moment I realized I was no longer under the law that I realized I was under grace. God's law is perfect and holy, but it has no power to make you perfect and holy. It is like a mirror; it shows mankind all of our imperfections. That's it's job. This does not mean we throw the baby out with the bath water. The law has its place. Its purpose is to lead us to Christ. The law was our "tutor to lead us to Christ" (Galatians 3:24). I like what Paul told the church in Roman, "For sin shall not have dominion over you, for you are not under law **but under grace.**" Freedom from the law will cause you to be free from the power and dominion of sin.

This world places much stress on our lives. It burdens us down with work and daily routines. The one thing we need for our minds is peace. God's rest gives us the ability to keep going. Hebrews 4:11 tells us, "Let us, therefore, make every effort to enter that rest..." God only wants us to make one effort, rest. How do we get more of the favor of God in our lives? Not by striving, only by diving into rest. How do we get more grace? Trust in what Christ has done for you on the Cross. When we rest, we are blessed.

(4) YOU ARE NOT ALONE

In the beginning of this book I asked the question, "How can grace be multiplied? I want to share with you another way grace can abound. Keep in mind this is not a positive way to get grace or a path we should pursue. Yet it should give us all hope that God's grace shines even in the darkness. Paul once told the church in Rome, "... **But where sin abounded, grace abounded much more,**" (Romans 5:20). Many times, when we sin. We feel that God is far away from us. Yes, sin does separate us from God, but because of the Cross we can now have fellowship with God. When you fall in a big pit, you're going to need a big rope. Where sin abounds, grace abounds all the more. Wow, that is amazing!

Even in our darkest moments, God is there. When we have failed and feel emotions of guilt and shame, God is whispering, "My grace is greater!" Many times we think that when a corporate executive or a leader sins, the news is quick to say that he, "fell from grace." Yet according to this verse in Romans where sin abounds, grace abounds much more! **When you sin, you do not fall from grace, you fall into grace.** This does not mean we should purposely sin, it does mean that

God is greater than our struggles. Here is a Dad joke for you, why doesn't Jesus wear jewelry? Because he breaks every chain!

The book of Proverbs tells us, "For a righteous man falls seven times, and rises again…" (Proverbs 24:16). How do you see yourself today? **Why does a righteous man get back up? Because he knows who he is.** I believe there is an abundance of grace for us today. It is time to realize it. When we sin and are in our darkest moments, that is when God picks us up. When Adam and Eve sinned, God did not stay away from them. Instead he went after them and said, "Where are you? (Genesis 3:9). Again when Cain sinned and killed his brother, God went after him. God spoke and said, "Where is your brother?" (Genesis 4:9). Time and time throughout the Bible God's grace abounded when people sinned.

This word for abound is two Greek words in one. The first is the word, "huper" which is where we have the English word, "hyper." The next word is, "Pleonazo" this simply means, "abundant or to increase." When we have the two words, we can see this as, "huperperisseuo" which means, "to abound beyond measure, to abound exceedingly, or to superabound."

It can be easy to magnify sin, but God wants us to magnify His grace. Yes, you may fall, and you may make a mistake, but you have to get back up. In the moments where we feel alone in a deep pit of sin, God is throwing us a rope of grace to pick us up. Stand back up and remember, that sin is not your identity any longer.

(5) YOU ARE A PART OF THE DOUBLE PORTION

There are five references of a positive double portion in the Bible. The first mention of the double portion is about the firstborn. Deuteronomy 21:17 tells us, "But he shall acknowledge **the firstborn,** the son of the unloved, by giving him **a double portion** of all that he has, for he is the beginning of his strength; to him belongs the right of the firstborn." A firstborn was entitled to have twice the inheritance so that he would be able to provide for his family. Jesus is **"the firstborn of all creation"** (Colossians 1:15). We are blessed because Christ has the double blessing of God.

The next mention is about Hannah. Because she could not have children, Hannah's husband tried to help her grief with an extra blessing. "But to Hannah he gave **a double portion, because he loved her"** (1 Samuel 1:5). We have a double portion in Christ **because God loves us.**

The third mention of the double portion is in the story of Job. Despite all his tragedy, it was the Lord who, "…restored the fortunes of Job, when he had prayed for his friends. And **the Lord gave Job twice as much as he had before."** (Job 42:10)

(ESV). Why does God want us to be blessed? So we can bless others. May your cup runneth over and into someone else's.

Another mention of the double portion is in the story of Elijah. He asked his mentor, "Ask what I shall do for you before I am taken from you." And Elisha said, "Please, let a double portion of your spirit be upon me." (2 Kings 2:9). While Elisha was not the physical son of Elijah, he was in a way Elijah's adopted son. Normally the father gives the doubles portion to the oldest son. Perhaps Elijah was looking around saying, "I don't own anything. What can I give to my Elisha?" Yet it was not about getting a physical item it was about a double anointing. Elisha asked for a double portion of his mentors spirit because **it is the Holy Spirit that brings the double portion.** Guess what, Elisha got the double anointing and did twice as many miracles as Elijah did. My friends may your children have a double portion of your kindness. You may say, "I don't have any money", give them a double portion of your kindness, joy, and love.

The final mention of the double portion is found in Isaiah 61:7 which says, "...Instead of your shame you shall have double honor..." (NKJV). Jesus is the true firstborn of God. He took our shame on the cross so that we can share in His double inheritance. If we count up everything we have in Christ, I think it could be safe to say that **we are twice as blessed we realize.**

(6) YOU ARE A FRIEND OF GOD

Proverbs 3:5-6 tells us, "Trust in the Lord with all your heart And do not lean on your own understanding. 6 In all your ways acknowledge Him, And He will make your paths straight." It is important to trust the Lord as we make decisions. Instead of trusting your intelligence, God wants to, "acknowledge Him."

The Hebrew word translated, "acknowledge" is the word, "yada`." I'm sure we all know someone who speaks with many words and sometimes it may sound like is yada, yada, yada. Strong's Lexicon defines this word as, "to know." In all that we do, we are called to know God. He directs our paths, but He does not control our path.

Psalms 23 explains how God takes care of us. In this chapter, we are told how He, "...is my shepherd...**He makes** me lie down in green pastures; **He leads** me...**He restores** my soul; He guides me..." (Psalms 23:1-3). On and on we are told of how the Lord protects us.

Yet notice what happens when I walk. "Even though I walk through the valley of the shadow of death, I fear no evil, for You are with me..." (Psalms 23:4). Psalms 23 turns from, "He leads me" to, "I walk." Where does He lead us? Beside the still waters and by the green pastures. Where do I walk? "Through the valley of the shadow of death." Notice this valley, was not guided by God. It is easy to lean on our own knowledge and strength, but it is vital to rely on the Lord's wisdom.

What does it mean to know God? To some, God sits far away in heaven, has a white beard, and is ready to judge us as soon as we fail. The truth is that God walks with us. Keep this in mind, "…God is love" (1 John 4:8). He is the essence of what we need in this life. In the Baker's Evangelical Dictionary of Biblical Theology, Carl Schultz wrote, "To know is not to be intellectually informed about some abstract principle, but to apprehend and experience reality[1]."

Knowing God is not about having knowledge of Him in an impersonal way. **To really know God is to walk with Him.** When you know His heart, you will trust the path of God. Believe that He will cause you to be at the right place at the right time. Give this year to God, and allow Christ to direct your path.

---

[1] Schultz, Carl. "Know, Knowledge - Baker's Evangelical Dictionary of Biblical Theology Online." *Bible Study Tools*. Bible Study Tools, n.d. Web. 02 Jan. 2017. <http://www.biblestudytools.com/dictionaries/bakers-evangelical-dictionary/know-knowledge.html>.

(7) YOU ARE REDEEMED

If you take time to study the tabernacle of Moses, you can see pictures of the cross throughout. Today we do not have a physical tabernacle. As believers, we are the temple of the Holy Spirit. When they made the temple, they had standing boards made from acacia wood, covered them with gold and placed them on top of silver sockets (see Exodus 26:15). The standing boards represent you and I as believers. We were all once trees in the dusty desert. **God took us and made us into a, "new creation" (2 Corinthians 5:17).** Gold in the Bible can be seen as righteousness. He then caused us to stand upright and covered us with righteousness (gold). He then takes us and places us on redemption ground (silver sockets).

Silver in the Bible can be seen to represent redemption. Jesus was sold by His own disciple, His own friend, for, "thirty pieces of silver" (Mathew 26:15). When we think about the cross, we can see how Jesus gave his life as a payment for our sin. God cannot just sweep sin under the carpet; it must be dealt with. Paul wrote that, "For the wages of sin is death, but the free gift of God is eternal life in Christ Jesus our Lord." (Romans 6:23). Sin is the anchor that pulls you down and causes you to drown. Jesus fully paid for the wages we owed.

C.H. Spurgeon once said, "What was the foundation of the Temple? It was the rock of Mount Moriah. And what was the hill of Moriah but the place where in many lights redemption and atonement had been illustrated." Mount Moriah was the mountain where Abraham was going to sacrifice his son Isaac to God. This was never God's conclusion, but it was used as a test. God provided a ram caught in the bushes to be the sacrifice. In the same way, we can look at the cross and see how Jesus became the ultimate sacrifice on the cross for our sins.

Ephesians 1:7 tells us, "⁷In Him we have redemption through His blood, the forgiveness of our trespasses, according to the riches of His grace." **We have redemption. We are not trying to earn it or gain it.** It is something we have freely through Jesus. 1 Corinthians 3:11 tells us, "For no man can lay a foundation other than the one which is laid, which is Jesus Christ." The place where you are standing is a place that has been bought with a high price; it is precious ground. You have been redeemed through the cross. Write this down on a notecard, declare it in the mirror, and speak it to your fellow believers. Wake up knowing you are standing on redemption ground!

(8) YOU ARE VICTORIOUS

Imagine being in a foreign country and serving time in prison. Your sentence is ten years, but your friend who loves you steps in and serves the ten years for you. You are able to walk free. Now although you are free you may feel a bit uncomfortable knowing your friend is taking the penalty for you. Image after many years you see your friend walk free. He is walking in peace because the payment has been completed. If you did not see him walk free, it would mean that he was likely still in bondage. In a similar way, Jesus on the Cross became sin, by died, and was in the grave for three days. If He never escaped the grave, we would have no hope. Thankfully Christ rose again and is still alive today!

Christ is a victor, and so are you. 2 Corinthians 2:14 tells us, "14 **But thanks be to God, who always leads us in triumph** in Christ..." The very fact that Jesus has been raised from the dead is a great message that He is victorious!

In the book *Sit, Walk, Stand*, Watchman Nee does a great job at explaining the book of Ephesians. He breaks the book into three parts, how we are seated with Christ in Heavenly places. The next part deals with how we walk with Christ. And the final chapters explain how we are called to stand in the armor of God. He explains, "By the resurrection God proclaimed his Son, victor over the whole realm of darkness, and the ground Christ won he has given to us...**Thus we do not fight *for* victory; we fight *from* victory**...Because victory is his, therefore it is ours." What is the ground we are standing on today? It is victory ground!

When the Scriptures talk about spiritual warfare in Ephesians 6:10-18 the word, "wrestle" appears once, yet the word, "stand" appears four times. Based on this I believe that spiritual warfare is 80% defensive and 20% offensive. Yes, there are battles and struggles that we face daily, but the Scriptures tell us, "...greater is He who is in you than he who is in the world." (1 John 4:4). I don't seek out the devil. That is not my calling in life. I am called to seek after God. When some people think about spiritual warfare, they have this idea that they need to go out and find darkness. I would not make that the goal. Instead seek after God, then when you encounter darkness, you will be able to stand strong.

Greg Laurie once said, "**Death died when Christ rose.**" Jesus, through the cross, has defeated death. The Apostle Paul once said, "...Where, O death, is your sting?" (1 Corinthians 15:55) (NIV). How can we have no fear of death ? The answer is one word, Jesus. When Christ rose from the dead, we rose with Him! **Christ is victorious, and so are you!**

(9) YOU ARE ALIVE

The Apostle Paul once said, "I have been crucified with Christ and I no longer live, but Christ lives in me. The life I now live in the body, I live by faith in the Son of God, who loved me and gave himself for me." (Galatians 2:20). What I love about this verse is how it is in past tense. Notice how the words, "I have." This speaks of something that has been done. When you finish paying your car off, you stop sending payments to the bank. You say, "I have paid my vehicle off." We are not waiting to enjoy our abundant life, we can have it today!

It is all about the cross. Christ was crucified in my place, so that I can live. He was crucified, and I was crucified. He rose again, and I rose with him! Of course, I wasn't literally there and didn't die physically, Christ was my substitute.

Think about baptism for a minute. When a person is baptized, they are symbolically buried with Christ (they go under the water), and they are raised with Christ (they rise out of the water). Keep in mind, we don't have to be baptized four or five times. We have been crucified with Christ once. We don't have keep going back into the water each time we sin because it was a payment, "Once and for all" (Hebrews 10:10).

The moment you believe in Christ, you are forgiven and set free. What were we freed from? We were freed from the punishment of sin. All of our sin was placed upon Jesus. Remember Jesus isn't going to die again, so He made one payment of sin, **"once and for all"** (1 Peter 3:18). He died and the sin went with him, but when He rose again the sin wasn't with Him. Romans 6:11 tells us, "Even so consider yourselves to be dead to sin, but alive to God in Christ Jesus." The Bible wants us to consider our new identity. Consider who you are in Christ. This word for, "sin" in this verse is actually a noun. We were once in bondage to sin. Now Christ has redeemed us from that cell.

Galatians 2:20 does not say we were crucified and stayed dead. That's only part of the story. This verse is saying that we were crucified, and now we are alive with Christ! Like water baptism, we're crucified at the cross and we're raised with Him. Christ took our bondage so that we can take His freedom.

(10) YOU ARE FORGIVEN

Colossians 2:13 tells us, "When you were dead in your transgressions and the uncircumcision of your flesh, He made you alive together with Him, **having forgiven us all our transgressions**," This forgiveness is something that we have. Because of the cross, God is able to righteously forgive and cleanse us of our sins. The ball is now in our court. Do you receive what he has done? The gospel is about faith through grace. God is not withholding forgiveness from us until we do enough good deeds. It is a gift of grace. When we believe in God, He saves us and we are forgiven.

What causes us to live a holy life? 2 Peter 1:5-9 give an amazing list of character qualities such as: diligence, moral excellence, knowledge, self-control, perseverance, godliness, brotherly kindness, and love. As Peter writes these amazing attributes, he also explains how to get them. In verse nine he says, "For he who lacks these *qualities* is blind *or* short-sighted, **having forgotten** *his* **purification from his former sins**."

Now what is the reason some do not have these great qualities? Because they have forgotten that they have been forgiven from their sins. God is constantly cleansing us from our sin. We are set free when we know we have been forgiven.

Peter is ultimately saying, "stop living in the past." Out of all of the disciples, he would have had a hard time forgiving himself. Here he had denied Jesus multiple times and had to realize God's true heart. He realized that God had forgiven him. That is what changed his life and that is what will change your life!

Should we still confess our sins? Yes, I believe that we should be open about our life towards God. Living Christ-conscious does not mean we deny our faults. It means that when we fall we take our eyes and look towards our savior. He has his hands outstretched and ready to pick us up. Pastor Timothy Keller once said, **"For every one look at your sin, take five looks at your savior."**

Feelings of guilt are natural when you sin. When we sin, we hurt God. He corrects us through the word and wants us to be free from condemnation. I don't confess my sins to be forgiven, **I confess my sins because I have already been forgiven**. Colossians explains how we have been forgiven of, "all" sins. I believe that all means all. Jesus paid one sacrifice for our sins.

Does this mean we can live any way that we want? No, this is what 2 Peter 1:9 is telling us. Peter is saying that when we are aware of God's forgiveness, we will live a holy life. What causes us to have self-control, moral excellence, and godliness? Knowing your identity in Christ and how you are completely forgiven.

(11) YOU ARE CLEAN

In the early 1500s, a young boy would go to church every Sunday staring at an image. This was a painting of Jesus with a frown on His face. This young boy could not get this away from His thoughts. He could only imagine standing one day before a Jesus with a frown on His face.

As this boy grew older he was at the, "Holy Stairs" on his knees praying and desiring remission of sins. It is believed that these were the same stairs Jesus walked up towards Pilate's house in Jerusalem. Yet they were relocated in Rome. He had this idea that if he punished himself through penance, God might be pleased with him. Yet as he is climbing the stairs the verse in the book of Romans kept ringing in his mind, "The just shall live by faith." (Romans 1:27). He keeps going. That phrase, "The just shall live by faith" was there again. As he gets to the middle of the stairs, he stopped and stood up. He climbed back down to the bottom, and he returned to Germany. This man was Martin Luther, the one who started the protestant reformation.

God made a balance transfer. We were bankrupt with no way to pay the penalty of sin. Christ was the one who never sinned. Yet on the cross, He became sin. He transferred our sin for His righteousness. Sin was punished so that we might be free.

There is something about being justified by faith that radically changes our lives. It is because He is holy that He will never impute sin towards you. He did not just sweep our sins under the rug, He fully paid the penalty of sin on the cross. Some things we do can hurt God, and not everything we do is pleasing to God. Yet we can know in our hearts that there is no condemnation in Christ. When we fail, we can go to God and speak to Him.

The empty tomb is God's way of telling us, our sins have been removed. The amazing part about your relationship with God is that not only are your sins forgiven, they are also sent away from you. When John the Baptist was baptizing people preaching about how there would be a savior, he said, **"Behold, the Lamb of God who takes away the sin of the world!"** (John 1:29). Knowing this truth will change the way you view God.

No longer do we have to live a life thinking God is frowning on us. We don't have to crawl on our knees in penance. God is pleased with you! Why? Faith pleases the Lord. When we place our faith in Christ as our savior, our sins are removed. "As far as the east is from the west, So far has He removed our transgressions from us." (Psalm 103:12). We are justified not by punishing ourselves but because Christ was punished on our behalf.

(12) YOU ARE BLESSED

Romans 4:7-7 tells us, "just as David also speaks of the blessing on the man to whom God credits righteousness apart from works: 7 "Blessed are those whose lawless deeds have been **forgiven**, and whose sins have been **covered**. 8 "Blessed is the man whose sin **the Lord will not take into account**." In this passage David mentions three attributes of a blessed man. A man is blessed when their sin is forgiven, covered, and remembered no more. We have covered these first two in the last chapters, now let's ask the question, does God keep an account of my sin as a Christian?

Exodus 34:7 tells us, "...He (God) will by no means leave the guilty unpunished, visiting the iniquity of fathers on the children and on the grandchildren to the third and fourth generations." Under the old covenant God would remember the sins of the fathers.

Sour wine is a picture of the generational curse. Ezekiel and Jeremiah talk about a saying that people had during the old covenant which reads, "The fathers eat the sour grapes, But the children's teeth are set on edge". According to the American Heritage Dictionary to set someone's teeth on edge means, "Something that one finds intensely irritating". This was a metaphor explaining how the sins of the father were passed down to the children. Here's where this gets interesting, during Jesus' crucifixion He was offered wine twice during the cross. The first wine was to ease the pain, almost as a way to numb what was happening. According to David Mathis the second wine was something that would have kept the criminal, "conscious for as long as possible". John 19:30 tells us, "Therefore when Jesus had received the sour wine, He said, "It is finished!" And He bowed His head and gave up His spirit." One of the very last things Jesus did for you during the cross was redeem you from all generational curses!

There are still consequence for our actions, and many habits that our parents have done can carry over. As far as judgement, your sin is removed. I believe that God still knows what we have done, but He does not bring it up. As Christians there are no generational curses, but we still struggle with generational habits and mindsets.

How can a holy, just, and righteous God not count our sins against us? Because they were counted at the cross. How can God remember our sins no more? Because they were remembered on the cross. We have what David longed for. We are the blessed man that David once spoke about. We are blessed because our sin is forgiven, covered, and remembered no more!

(13) YOU ARE WONDERFULLY MADE

If you were flying in a plane over a deserted island and as you came across a portion of the island, you saw on the sand rocks in formation of the letters, "H-E-L-P." By seeing the rocks in order, you would assume that there is someone down there that is in need. Perhaps you turn toward the co-pilot and say, "Look there on the beach those rocks spell out help." We better radio the coast guard and investigate. And if your co-pilot said, "oh you know the waves must have just thrown the rocks in that order. There is no one down there. Those rocks are there because the random placement of the water." Now the word, "help" is a very simple design. Now even in this simple design we recognize intelligence. Surely when it comes to much more complex designs it is irrational to deny the truth that there is a creator.

Here are some neat facts about our body. Nerve impulses sent from the brain move at a speed of 274 km/h. According to the *Telegraph*, "The human brain has a capacity that is ten times greater than first thought and can retain 4.7 billion books." And did you know that, our bones are about five times stronger than steel. The human body is amazing.

You are no accident. You did not get here by a random chance. You have been placed on this Earth for a purpose. The Bible says, "For You formed my inward parts; You wove me in my mother's womb. I will give thanks to You, for **I am fearfully and wonderfully made**; Wonderful are Your works, And my soul knows it very well." (Psalms 139:13-14).

This word, "made" explains to us how we have designed. Just as an architect makes the blueprint of a building, God has done the same for you. Ken Ham, the president of Answers in Genesis, once said, "What you believe about who you are, where you came from, affects your whole worldview." Knowing our identity in Christ and how we have been wonderfully made has a strong impact on our life. What does it mean to be fearfully made? I love Barnes' commentary on this verse, he looks at the Hebrew and reinterprets the sentence to say, "I am distinguished by things in my creation which are suited to inspire awe." We are made so wonderfully that it causes us to stand in awe and worship God!

Allow God to continue to knit your life. Seek the Lord and allow Him to give you wisdom. Sometimes we think that if we give God the steering wheel of our life we will end up as a missionary in Africa. There are many whom God has called into this field, but remember that God can use you right where you are. Sometimes we are called to bloom where we are planted. Think about this, If He can form your physical body, why not allow Him to guide and form your life? Lee Strobel, author of *the Case for Christ*, once said, "I think people who believe that life emerged naturalistically need to have a great deal more faith than people who reasonably infer that there's an Intelligent Designer."

This book was not formed by accident. I thought about each word and sentence. It is here because there was a creator. In the same way, you are here because there is a Creator. I tell you this because God wants you to know that you are loved. He wants you to know that you have been fearfully and wonderfully made. How many times would a creator die for His creation? Not many, and yet you are so important to God that He gave His life for you!

(14) YOU ARE FREE

When the Emancipation Proclamation was signed by Abraham Lincoln, all American slaves were freed. It had been two and a half years since this executive order had been issued. Yet there were documented cases where some slave owners tried to hide this news, and slaves remained in bondage because they didn't know they were free. According to the National Public Radio, "Maj. Gen. Gordon Granger arrived in Galveston, Texas, with 2000 troops and a message - slaves were free."

Many slaves were held in bondage because the news was hidden. In a similar way, I believe the enemy is doing the same thing today. He wants to hide this knowledge that you have been made a new creation in Christ. I'm here to proclaim the news to you, today because of the cross you are made completely new! You are no longer a slave to sin, but you are a child of the King! Now walk in the freedom you already have!

Michael Angelo once said, "I saw the angel in the marble and carved until I set free." **God wants to see you living in freedom.** Sometimes we do not see ourselves the way God does. It's time to put on our grace glasses and see who we are. Because of the cross,

God has taken away all of the gunk and sin that held our wings down. Don't hold on to what God removed. Stand tall knowing what He has done.

After Moses came down the mountain with the ten commandments. The Israelites had made a golden calf and were worshiping it. The Scriptures tell us, "On the next day Moses said to the people, "You yourselves have committed a great sin; and now I am going up to the Lord, **perhaps I can make atonement for your sin.**" (Exodus 32:30). Notice the tone that Moses has. He said, "perhaps I can make atonement". He did not have confidence in his ability to make atonement. Yet when Jesus went to the Cross, He knew with certainty He would be able to do it. 1 John 2:2 says, "**He is the atoning sacrifice for our sins**, and not only for ours but also for the sins of the whole world." For everyone who believes, Jesus is our atonement!

Sometimes it is a lack of knowledge that can keep us defeated. Because of the Cross, we have been set free from the bondage of sin. **The gospel of grace is not filled with words like perhaps or maybe. Instead it is spoken with a definite yes!** John 8:36 tells us, "So if the Son sets you free, you will be free indeed." (ESV). It's time to walk in the freedom we have in Christ!

(15) YOU ARE GOD'S MASTERPIECE

Michelangelo once said, "Every block of stone has a statue inside it and it is the task of the sculptor to discover it." In life, there are times when it feels like we hit a wall. Everything is going great and then, bam! We are looking at a block of stone in front of us. What do we do? How are we to respond? Maybe we blame God saying, "God why have you allowed this to happen?" Maybe we complain and become bitter about it. In these moments of defeat, remember that God can take that wall and turn it into a work of art. Take the time and energy that you have and allow God to sculpt your life.

Simply because something is negatively affecting you does not mean that God caused it. Some believe that, "Everything happens for a reason" and that, "What will be will be." Yet if Moses would not have lifted His hands and stuck the water, would the Red Sea have parted? If Noah didn't build the Ark, would they have lived? And if David had not stepped out in faith, would he have killed the giant? Ultimately, we are faced with many challenges in this life. There is but one question, who will you turn to?

Jesus once said, "Come to Me, all who are weary and heavy-laden, and I will give you rest." (Mathew 11:28). God wants us to turn towards Him. I love the NIV Application Commentary on this passage which says, "...discipleship to Jesus is not essentially a religious obligation. Rather, ours is an intimate relationship with the One who calls, 'Come to me' and 'learn from me.'" Let us continue to place our care on Christ. Stop the endless cycle of fear and anxiety. Some things in life we cannot control. Do the best that you can do, pray, and give it to the Lord.

Sometimes we wait for the perfect opportunity or the perfect timing. Yet all the while we miss the good we can do right now. Let's not become so super-spiritual that we look past the here and now. When something doesn't go our way, what will be our response? Are we going to take a step of faith and trust God? Or will we sit still and do nothing?

Maybe you lost your job, got sick, or was in a car wreck. Take time to grieve. Allow God to minister to you. Yet remember that this can be an opportunity to take the time you have and make something great. Don't allow depression to have its way. Inside every negative situation is a statue that can be carved out. Keep moving forward. Use your time and energy to turn what was meant for your harm to work out for your good. You hold the carving tools. Take them and place them in the God's hands, the perfect sculptor. Discover the statue in every stony situation.

(16) YOU ARE NOT CONDEMNED

Romans 8:1 tells us, "There is now no condemnation for those who are in Christ Jesus." These words, "no condemnation" echo our freedom in Christ. Notice the present tense in the word, "now". This verse is telling us that, "There is now no condemnation" it is speaking of the very present place we are in. **This no condemnation is not just for heaven, it is here at this hour.**

What does it mean to be in Christ? To be in Christ means that we receive His sacrifice as payment for our sins. Once you believe in Jesus, you are placed in Christ. Some may think that there is no condemnation for those who obey God. But that makes no sense. It is because we have fallen, that we need this grace. We do not earn our place in Chris. It is a gift.

When a building is condemned, it is unfit for use. The doors are locked, the windows are boarded up, and it is a hopeless place. When people are under condemnation, they literally feel unfit for use. They feel hopeless and unworthy. My friend, God declares you fit for use. This is the whole message of the gospel! He has declares that you are a, "…new creation. The old has passed away; behold, the new has come." (2 Corinthians 5:17) (ESV).

Some people try to get rid of a problem by focusing on the fruit. The truth is, we have to take care of the root. If the root is bad so will the fruit be. One of the main root causes of our problems is condemnation. Somewhere we are still bringing up the past about a sin. When you

God declares you fit for use!

have a small pebble in your shoe, it affects your walk. This is what it is like to walk around in condemnation.

Think about a fresh piece of pine wood. It is a great piece of wood. I can smell it right now. It is what holds your typical house together. Yet if you take this piece of wood, neglect it and leave it outside. It will begin to rot and warp. Stay protected under the wings of the Almighty. Don't let the negative rain of this world cause your heart to warp. Keep it protected. If you base your value on who people say you are, your life will be like a roller coaster, up one day and down the next.

It is time to be free and receive no condemnation. My Mom (Shelley Gibson) once said, "When you know who you are, you will have victory over the enemy!" Christ was punished for us so that we would not be punished. You are in Christ! God no longer condemns you, so do not condemn yourself.

(17) YOU ARE A LIGHT

In a period of silence where there had been over four hundred years without no prophet or new Scripture, a small baby is born. Two thousand years later, we are still talking about Him. There is something amazing about how even the darkest nights can be lit up. We are called to be a light to this world.

Daniel 12:3 tells us, "Those who are wise will **shine like the brightness of the heavens,** and those who lead many to righteousness, **like the stars for ever and ever.**" God wants you to shine bright. When I think of people who are wise they shine bright at what they are knowledgeable in. I love listening to John Campea or Collider Movie Talk speak about Star Wars. Why? Because they are knowledgeable about what they are talking about. Have you ever been around someone passionate about something? There is something so amazing that causes us to be more interested. May we all have a passion for Christ that causes us to shine bright.

The Star of Bethlehem was not just a normal star. It was a star that even Astronomers from the East noticed it. The star had a simple part to play. It pointed to the place where our Savior was born.

May we all be like the Star of Bethlehem and point people to Christ. Matthew 5:14-16 tells us, **"You are the light of the world.** A city set on a hill cannot be hidden; [15] nor does *anyone* light a lamp and put it under a basket, but on the lampstand, and it gives light to all who are in the house. [16] **Let your light shine** before men in such a way that they may see your good works, and glorify your Father who is in heaven." Our life is a witness to others. How we carry ourselves, respond to adversity, and treat other people will effect our witness. When we choose to smile and have a good attitude we are being a light.

May we all be like a lighthouse. A lighthouse warns boats on the ocean that they are too close to the shore. If a boat does not know where the shore is, they could crash. The lighthouse serves as a beacon to guide the boats during a foggy night. Many people can live in a fog. We can get overwhelmed with fogs of stress, anxiety, and worry. May we be a lighthouse and guide them closer to the shore. Only the Holy Spirit is able to lift that fog from their lives. We just point them in the right direction.

God wants us to shine like the stars. **May your life be light for others!** It's time to recognize that God's light shines even in the darkness. Let's begin to look at how wonderful Jesus it. I believe that this is what God has called us to do. We are all called to reflect the light that God has given to us.

(18) YOU ARE A NEW CREATION

Scripture tells us, "Therefore, if anyone *is* in Christ, **he is a new creation**; old things have passed away; behold, all things have become **new**." (2 Corinthians 5:17) (NKJV). This reality is not about how good you are; it is a simple question, are you in Christ? If you believe in Jesus then the answer is a definite yes! It does not say, "well maybe" or, "I hope so". No, this is a fact. You are a new creation!

You may say, "How am I a new creation if I still have a sinful nature?" Being a new creation is not about your physical appearance or your actions, it is about faith. It is by God's unmerited favor through our faith that we are changed. To fully understand our new identity, we must know how we have three parts. You have a spirit, soul, and a body. The soul is best defined as your mind, will and emotions. **Your spirit is new, your mind is being renewed, and your body will be made new one day.**

Let's look at Romans 13:14 which says" Rather, clothe yourselves with the Lord Jesus Christ, and do not think about how to grat-ify the desires of the sinful nature." (NIV). According to this verse, we have two natures, but when we read Galatians 5:24 it tells us something else, "**Those who belong to Christ Jesus have cruci-fied the sinful nature** with its passions and desires." See the confusion? One says we have a sinful nature and the other says we do not. This idea of a sinful nature derives from the NIV translation of the Bible. Now I want to clarify that I believe the NIV is a great translation of the Bible, and I have given it to others as gifts. The reason this began here is because the NIV is written on a 3rd grade reading level. It's written in a way that many people can pick it up and understand it without all of the Old English, "thees" and "thous." When we look at these Scriptures we can see how this word is used, "sinful nature," but in the Greek this is actually the word, "sarx" which means, "flesh." When the translators of the NIV Bible got to this word, instead of saying, "flesh" they translated it as "sinful nature" to help the reader.

When Dr. Andrew Farley wrote about this in one of his books, Zondervan was actually the publisher, the same company that makes the NIV translation of the Bible. They exchanged emails about this, and I'm sure there are others that brought this to their attention. In 2011 when Zondervan printed their Bibles, in most cases, they actually corrected this translation. They simply interpreted the word sarx as, "flesh" and let people interpret it for themselves.

What is this, "flesh" that we wage war against? The flesh is, "the worldly way to feel okay." According to *HELPS – word studies* the word sarx is, "is generally negative, referring to making decisions (actions) *according to self* – i.e. done *apart from faith."* When you walk according to the flesh you are walking in the world's ways. **The flesh is the world's ways to earn acceptance.** God's ways are much different, we operate by faith.

As Dr. Farley says, "We need to get rid of that, yin yang theology," the idea that we are old and new. Our old self was crucified with Christ. You do not have a sinful nature. Yes we face temptation, but that battle is in our mind not our nature. God has given us a new nature and Godly desires. If you sin, remind yourself that this is not who you are, that is not your identity. It's time to be the man/woman God has called you to be. You are not a house divided. **You are made completely new through the cross!**

(19) YOU ARE THE ONE

My church partnered up with Discover Life Church, a local church in our area. We have been having LIT (Leaders In Training) once a year for Junior High and High School students. This is a three-day event with worship, a word, food, and games. At one of our leadership meetings, preparing for the event, Pastor Jonathon Salas gave a great example. He said, "We need to have the, 'I'm the one' attitude." What does this mean? Is there a spill on the floor? **I'm the one** to clean it. Is there someone standing away from the group, disinterested in what is going on? **I'm the one** to go and encourage him. Is there someone struggling to carry an ice chest? **I'm the one** to help them. When we have this attitude, God is happy. It's the same mindset that set Jesus apart from everyone around Him. Jesus served one person at a time.

2 Chronicles 16:9 tells us, "For the eyes of the LORD move to and fro throughout the earth that He may strongly support those whose heart is completely His..." This verse tells us how God is looking for someone to be used for His kingdom. He is not looking for simple behavior modification, He wants heart transformation.

D. L. Moody is one of the great preachers of the 1800s. Throughout his life he made a huge impact on many people's lives. He was like the Billy Graham of his day. He opened up universities still open today. Along D. L. Moody's path there were many people who made an impact into his personal journey with God. One day Moody was sitting with his friend Harvey, a British revivalist, recounting a private conversation a year ago. Although Harvey did not remember saying these exact words Moody explained that this was what God had spoken through him. He recalls him saying, "Moody, **the world has yet to see what God will do with a man fully consecrated to him!**" Dwight made a decision in his heart when he heard those words that, "By the grace of God, I am that man." Dwight went on to reach millions with the gospel of Christ. All of this happened because one man said, "God don't look any further, I'll be your voice[2]."

Have the, "I'm the one" attitude. Remind yourself that, "I am the one God Loves! I am the one God has Forgiven! And I am the one Jesus died for!" Live a life that is, "LIT!" Live your life being a light to this world. Spread the good news! There is purpose in your life!

---

[2] https://www.christianitytoday.com/history/issues/issue-25/world-has-yet-to-see.html

(20) YOU ARE VALUABLE

A speaker once started off his seminar by holding up a $20 bill. In the room of 200, he asked. "Who would like this $20 bill?" Hands started going up. He said, "I am going to give this $20 to one of you - but first, let me do this." He proceeded to crumple the twenty dollar note up. He then asked. "Who still wants it?" Still the hands were up in the air.

"Well," he replied, "what if I do this?" He dropped it on the ground and started to grind it into the floor with his shoe. He picked it up, now crumpled and dirty. "Now, who still wants it?" Still the hands went into the air.

"My friends, you have all learned a very valuable lesson. No matter what I did to the money, you still wanted it because it did not decrease in value. It was still worth $20. Many times in our lives, we are dropped, crumpled, and ground into the dirt by the decisions we make and the circumstances that come our way. We feel as though we are worthless; but no matter what happened or what will happen, you will never lose your value."

Jesus once said, "Look at the birds of the air, that they do not sow, nor reap nor gather into barns, and yet your heavenly Father feeds them. Are you not worth much more than they?" (Matthew 6:26). I love his attitude. He tells us to, "Look to the birds" and see how God provides for them. God is telling us today, "you are valuable!" Christ was explaining to them how they need to be worry free and trust God. I love how He said, "Are you not worth much more than they?" He has a desire to give us a, "hope and a future" (Jeremiah 29:11). Throughout the Bible God uses creation as an example.

How much should an artist charge for their painting? Whatever they think someone is willing to pay for it. In my opinion, no painting is worth $450 Million, but in New York of 2016 a man from Saudi Arabia thought a Leonardo da Vinci painting was worth it. When we try to understand our worth, we must remember Calvary. It cost a lot to purchase you from the slave market of sin. It cost Jesus His life.

If you find your worth in your finances, health, or relationship status, when you lose it you will feel empty. Depression will fill your mind because you feel a void. Many people place their whole identity in their relationship with their significant other. When the relationship fails, they lose their job, or get diagnosed with a sickness, they become hopeless. Now yes, we all will go through a level of sadness when something ends, but I'm here to give you a word of encouragement, look to the light. We have to understand that our identity is not in the things of this world; it is in Christ. Don't place your entire worth on these temporary things. **God wants you to place your hope in something that is eternal.**

Ask yourself this, "Where am I placing my hope?" Am I placing my worth on the sand of my abilities, or am I placing it on the immovable rock? Don't place your value in things that are temporary. Instead place your worth in something that is eternal. Because of the cross you are worthy to be a part of the kingdom. You are worthy to take communion. And you are worthy to stand before God as righteous!

Our worth is not measured by our bank account, health, or relationship status, it is measured by the cross. God's outstretched hands should send a message to your heart that says, "I'd rather die than live without you!"

(21) YOU ARE ROYALTY

The Scriptures defines God as the, "King of Kings." (1 Timothy 6:15). The greatest King to ever rule pales in comparison to Jesus. If you believe in Christ as your savior, you are born into the family of God. You are royalty.

Have you ever tried to study the Bible in a year? Maybe you started with Genesis, learned about Abraham, heard about the parting of the Red Sea, and saw how God delivered His people from Egypt. Then you get stuck in between some long genealogies. It's like how some movies begin by listing the main actors and filmmakers. Maybe you just watch it and are like, "Ok. ok, just get to the plot!" What we need to remember is that the genealogy of a King is very important. After the birth of Jesus, there is no more genealogies recorded in the Bible. Why not? Because the main purpose of genealogy was for the prophecy of Genesis 3:15 to become reality. After Adam and Eve sinned, God said that Eve's offspring would be bit on the heel, but He (Jesus) would, "crush" Satan's head. This took place through Jesus' death on the cross!

The movie, *Black Panther* deals with a villain who was heir to the throne and it was a battle for the Kingdom of Wakanda. In fact, many movies are around this idea of the throne. Why? Because it is important who is on the throne. Who are you allowing to influence your life and decisions?

Why does a diamond stand out compared to the rocks? **Because it shines and is rare.** It is uncommon. God gives us the church a crown of righteousness. Paul told young Timothy, "In the future there is laid up for me the crown of righteousness, which the Lord, the righteous Judge, will award to me on that day; and not only to me, but also to all who have loved His appearing." (2 Timothy 4:8) What a wonderful gift!

Kings and Queens are called to conduct their lives with dignity and honor. In a similar way, we are called to walk knowing who we are in Christ. Walk knowing you have been made right with God. Walk knowing God has crowned you with "glory and honor" (Hebrews 2:7). And walk knowing you're royalty because your Father God is the, "King of Kings!"

(22) YOU ARE A PURPLE PRIEST

"But you are a chosen generation, **a royal priesthood**, a holy nation, His own special people, that you may proclaim the praises of Him who called you out of darkness into His marvelous light" (1 Peter 2:9) (NKJV).

Notice the words, "royal priesthood". This speaks of how **we are royalty and are priests at the same time.** We see no one in the Bible who had a duel role of being a priest and a king. David, Saul, Solomon, Ahab and many others were kings, but they were not priests. Samuel, Nathan, and Aaron were priest but were not kings. A royal priesthood is very rare, and that is what you are in Christ. **You are rare!**

You are a purple priest. The color purple is known for the color of royalty. Evan Andrews, a writer for *the History Channel* said that before the 15th century, "Clothes made from the dye were exorbitantly expensive—a pound of purple wool cost more than most people earned in a year…"[3] Since we are royalty, we have a royal robe.

---

[3] https://www.google.com/amp/s/www.history.com/.amp/news/why-is-purple-considered-the-color-of-royalty

When Adam sinned, he realized that he was naked. Adam used fig leaves to cover himself. Later God then took an animal, had it killed, and took its fur to make a covering for Adam and Eve. In a similar way, Jesus is our covering. He is the Lamb of God who took away our sins. We are covered now in a, "robe of righteousness" (Isaiah 61:10).

Jesus was one of the few who was from the lineage of a king and after the priestly order of Melchizedek. The original priests were from the lineage of the tribe of Levi. God choose this tribe to work as priests for the entire nation. Yet this was not God's original plan. Before Israel worshiped the golden calf, God told them that He wanted Israel to be a, "kingdom of priests" (Exodus 19:3-6). Sadly, Israel could not keep God's law, and instead God used the tribe of Levi to become the priests. After this if you wanted to become a priest you had to be a Levite or else you could not be one. The role of a prophet was to represent God to the people. The role of the priest was to represent the people to God. If they had a good High Priest, the nation was blessed. If they had an bad High Priest, it had a negative effect on the people.

Revelation 1:6 says, "and **He has** made us to be a kingdom, priests to His God and Father-to Him be the glory and the dominion forever and ever. Amen." My good friend's Larry Martinez and Jamey Escamilla, have a great purpose for their ministry. They always want people to know why they believe in what they believe. We must know what we believe and be able to teach it.

What was the problem with the old covenant? There is nothing wrong with the law, it is perfect. The old covenant law is good. It is similar to how a mirror is, it shows us who we really are. The mirror (the old covenant) cannot make an ugly man handsome. Grace is the solution, and Jesus is grace personified. The old covenant was based on works. The priesthood of the law says, "If you…" The priesthood of grace says, "He has." He has made us righteous! He has made us holy! And He has made us a purple priest!

(23) YOU ARE AN EAGLE

A farmer tried to raise an eaglet among some chickens. The eaglet was taught to run around like a chicken and scratch the dirt like a chicken. Instead of flying, it was always taught to look down, and to run away from snakes like a scared chicken. But each time it did those things, it knew in its heart that something was wrong. One day, it happened to look up and see an eagle flying high and majestically in the sky, with a snake grasped in its claws! The eagle gave a loud shriek that resonated deep within the heart of the eaglet.

It tried to tell the chickens about it, but the chickens just said, "Stop dreaming! You're a chicken. We chickens are earth-bound. We don't fly. And we're terrified of snakes!" But the more the eaglet saw the eagle, the more it saw its true destiny. The sight and call of the eagle eventually captured its heart, so that finally, it was able to shut out the voices of unbelief, shake off its earth-bound mentality and take off to the skies to live the high life of an eagle!

When you were born again as a child of God, everything necessary for success, for being the head and not the tail, for being above only and not beneath, and for living the victorious life, was given to you. You may be around negative people, but you must rise above those thoughts and stay high. Keep seeing and meditating on your true identity in Christ—a beloved, righteous child of God destined to soar and reign in life. The more you get this into your heart, the more you'll be able to shut out the voices that try to keep you down and defeated.

The Scriptures tell us, "Although Moses was one hundred and twenty years old when he died, his eye was not dim, nor his vigor abated" (Deuteronomy 34:7). There was something spiritual that happened in the life of Moses that effected his physical body. Hebrews 11:27 tells us, "By faith he left Egypt, not fearing the wrath of the king; for he endured, as **seeing Him who is unseen**". How did Moses leave Egypt? He left by faith. I love Mathew Henry's Commentary on this passage, "There was no decay in the strength of his body, nor in the vigour and activity of his mind; his understanding was as clear, and his memory as strong as ever."

The last part of Hebrews 11:27 tells us that Moses was healthy even at the age of 120 because He kept seeing Him who is unseen. According to *One Kind Planet* an Eagles eyesight is 4-5 times greater than that of a human." There is true health and peace when you continue to look up. My friend, God calls us eagles, and He calls us to live the high life with Him. Keep your head up and remember that you are an eagle!

(24) YOU ARE ESTABLISHED

"In righteousness you will be established; You will be far from oppression, for you will not fear; And from terror, for it will not come near you." (Isaiah 54:14). God doesn't want us to just simply know about this, He wants us to be established in this new covenant truth. So why is righteousness important to know?

Knowing your identity in Christ is crucial because it effects our relationship with God. Your prayer life is directly effected by this. The more you are aware that you are righteous in Christ, the more you will pray. There is something about standing that is important. When Paul talked about the armor of God he talked about the need to stand firm.

Paul wrote, "Even so Abraham BELIEVED GOD, AND IT WAS RECKONED TO HIM AS RIGHTEOUSNESS." (Galatians 3:6). Now when did Abraham become righteous? Immediately, he believed, and God gave him righteousness. This word for reckoned is an accounting term. This means that God credited righteousness to our spiritual bank account. Righteousness is there for anyone; all they have to do is receive it. How was Abraham blessed? He was blessed by the Lord. Abraham was not blessed because of his works. As we read, "Now Abraham was old, well advanced in age; and the LORD had blessed Abraham in all things." (Gen. 24:1)[4]. Do you want to be blessed in all things? Then receive this free gift of righteousness.

According to the website, *GotQuestions.org*, "A typical armed soldier wore a breastplate made of bronze or chain mail. It covered the vital organs, namely, the heart, and was fitted with loops or buckles that attached it to a thick belt. If the belt was loosened, the breastplate slipped right off." The breastplate of righteousness guards one of the most important parts of our body, our heart. God wants us to protect our heart. How do we do this? By having peace knowing we are righteous in Christ.

Isn't it interesting that a thick belt used to be attached to this breastplate. It is the belt of truth that keeps our breastplate of righteousness on. There is power in knowing truth. **The more you are around Jesus the more you are around truth** because Jesus is, "the way, the truth, and the life" (John 14:6).

---

[4] NKJV

(25) YOU ARE A CITIZEN OF GOD'S KINGDOM

In 2018, Missionary Kenneth "J.R." Danforth went missing after their boat capsized off the coast of Tanzania in the Indian Ocean. He was never found. The last time Sam Cunningham saw his friend J.R., he asked him, "How does it feel to be home?" J.R. replied, "I don't know if Africa is my home now or Texas. I guess Heaven's my home." Those were Sam's last memories about him.

Perhaps we should have the same attitude. Maybe we should live like J.R. and know that our eternal home is not on Earth, it is in Heaven. The truth is that we are all foreigners in this land. The Disciple Peter once wrote, "Beloved, I urge you as aliens and strangers [in this world] to abstain from the sensual urges [those dishonorable desires] that wage war against the soul." (1 Peter 2:11) (Amplified Bible). According to this passage we are aliens in the world. Our life is now about bringing the kingdom of God to this Earth. May we live a life that causes people to see a glimpse into Heaven.

What will Heaven be like? While I cannot give you a total blueprint of what it will look like, I can tell you what it will sound like. Heaven will be filled with worship. True worship happens when our mind, will, and emotions and involved. Timothy Keller once said, "Worship is the act of ascribing ultimate value to something in a way that energizes and engages your entire being."

Psalms 95 gives us a description of this. It says, "O come, let us sing for joy to the Lord, Let us shout joyfully to the rock of our salvation...For the Lord is a great God And a great King above all gods...Come, let us worship and bow down, Let us kneel before the Lord our Maker." (Psalms 96:1,3,6). Verse one shows us how our emotions are involved in worship. It uses words such as, "sing, shout, thanksgiving." Also, in verse six we are called to worship with our will. It uses words such as, "come, kneel, bow down." Finally, in verse eight the language of reason and thinking is used.

Citizens typically adopt the culture, language, and lifestyle of the nation they belong to. To be a citizen of the Heaven means that we follow God's pattern for life. We are called to speak differently than those on this Earth, and we live not after the ways of this world.

Whether it was teaching, digging water wells, playing cards, or putting up a basketball goal J.R. gave his time to bring Heaven to Earth. May we all have a desire to use the resources that we have and make a difference! J.R. once said, **"The Gospel is so easy. Living for the Lord is so easy. Love people, follow the Spirit."**

(26) YOU HAVE A NEW NAME

During the reign of King Nebuchadnezzar, three men had to make a decision. In front of them stood a ninety-foot-tall idol made of gold. They were commanded to bow down and worship or be thrown into a fiery furnace. Maybe they were looking at each other and contemplating. Perhaps wondering what they should do next. They decide what to do despite the fear of death. Shadrach, Meshach, and Abednego stand up for their God and later tell the king, "...O Nebuchadnezzar, we do not need to give you an answer concerning this matter. 17 If it be so, our God whom we serve is able to deliver us from the furnace of blazing fire; and He will deliver us out of your hand, O king. 18 But even if He does not, let it be known to you, O king, that we are not going to serve your gods or worship the golden image that you have set up." (Daniel 3:16-17). These three men stood for what they believed in.

The king has them bound and thrown into the furnace which was heated seven time hotter than normal. The men who threw them in died from the heat of the flame. Yet even though they were knocked down and tied up, the Scriptures tell us that Nebuchadnezzar saw them standing up and, "...walking about in the midst of the fire without harm..." (Daniel 3:25). **No matter what fiery furnace you are going through, remember that God is standing with you.**

What caused Shadrach, Meshach, and Abednego to be so bold? I believe that it was because they knew their true names. Although these names sound great because they rhyme, when we look at their definition, these are really terrible names. We know them by Shadrach, Meshach, and Abednego, but these were not their original names. These were the names that King Nebuchadnezzar gave them.

You see King Nebuchadnezzar was a narcissistic king of Babylon. He conquered much territory, moved into Jerusalem, burned down the temple, and had taken captives. The Babylonian Empire was great at brainwashing people and mixing them into their culture. One of the ways they did this was by changing their names.

He took Hananiah (God is Gracious) and changed it to Shadrach (Commander of the moon God). He took Mishael (who is like God) to Meshach (Who is like the Moon God). And he took Azzuriah (God has helped) to Abednego (Servant of Nego).

Names are very important. Our enemy is called the, "accuser of the brethren" (Revelation 12:10). He is always trying to rename us. Don't allow it to happen. Don't allow your name to be sick, depressed, or sad. Take that identity and cast it aside. **Receive your new name**: beloved, favored, righteous, blessed, the head and not the tail, and servant of the Lord.

(27) YOU ARE NOT BORN TO LOSE

Dr. Norman Vincent Peale shares a great story from his book, *The Power of the Plus Factor*, "Once walking through the twisted little streets of Kowloon in Hong Kong, I came upon a tattoo studio. In the window were displayed samples of the tattoos available. On the chest or arms you could have tattooed an anchor or flag or mermaid or whatever. But what struck me with force were three words that could be tattooed on one's flesh, 'Born to Lose'. I entered the shop in astonishment and, pointing to those words, asked the Chinese tattoo artist, 'Does anyone really have that terrible phrase, Born to Lose, tattooed on his body?' He replied, 'Yes, sometimes.' 'But,' I said, 'I just can't believe that anyone in his right mind would do that.' The Chinese man simply tapped his forehead and in broken English said, 'Before tattoo on body, tattoo on mind.'"

What is on your mind today? Do you have a false name tattooed on your mind? What negative labels have you or other people given to you? You can't stop people from calling you names, but you must remember that you don't have to answer that name. Practice reverse gossip, say something great about someone behind their back.

You don't need a new situation; you need a new perspective. In Christ you are made new.

God changed many names in the Bible. For instance, He changed: Abram (High Father) to Abraham (Father of many), Sarai (Princess) to Sarah (Mother of Nations), Jacob (Supplanter) to Israel (having power with God), Simon (God has heard) to Peter (Rock), and Ben-oni to Benjamin. While the last name in this list was not directly changed by God, He still inspired it. **Names are important to God because they speak of our identity.** Typically, a person's favorite word in the dictionary is their name.

Now Jacob and Rachel had a great love for each other. Jacob worked fourteen years to marry her. They were of old age and finally were able to have a second son after losing Joseph (See Genesis 35:16-19). During the birth, Rachel suffered severely and was about to pass away. Before she died, she named their son, Ben-oni which means, "Son of my sorrow". Forever this child's name would have been spoken and remembered as a man of sorrow. "Hello sorrowful!" or "Hey what's for dinner man of sorrows" they would have called him.

> You don't need a new situation; you need a new perspective.

Rachel wanted to call the boy to be, "Son of my sorrow" but **Jacob instead called Him, "Son of my right hand."** I'm sure Jacob was going through an extremely difficult time. When I read the story,

I imagine him rising up and declaring with tears in his eyes, "My son will not be called sorrow. My son will be called, 'son of my right hand!'" It's time to remove those negative labels. You are valuable, greatly blessed, and a history maker!

The death of Rachel was a great tragedy for the family of Jacob. Rachel wanted to forever have her son remembered for the sorrow he brought. Thankfully Jacob was guided by the Lord and gave him a new name. Rachel died in Bethlehem, but this is where a greater Benjamin was born, Jesus. God brought salvation to Jacob's ancestors in the place of great tragedy. Isaiah 53:3 speaks of Jesus saying, "He is despised and rejected of men, a Man of sorrows..." **Jesus became Ben-oni on the cross so that we can become Benjamin today!**

Thankfully Benjamin lived a great life being a man of God and honoring his family. I believe this is because of his new name. God is giving you a new name today. You are not born to lose, you are born to win in life! Because of the cross you are not a son of sorrows, you are a daughter of destiny, a son of strength, and a child of victory!

(28) YOU ARE A WORLD CHANGER

There was once a man heading to the market with his grandson riding their donkey. They soon passed a group of men, one of them said: "See that lazy youngster, he lets his grandfather walk while he rides." So the man ordered the lad to get off, and got on himself. But they hadn't gone far when they passed two women, one of whom said to the other: "Shame on that lazy man to let the little kid trudge along."

Well, the man didn't know what to do, but at last he picked up his grandson and they both rode on the donkey. By this time they had come close to the town when they heard, "Aren't you ashamed of yourself for overloading that poor donkey?" The man and boy got off and ended up carrying the donkey into town.

No matter what you do, you are not going to please everyone. The world is trying to change us. They are trying to make us fit into their box and deny God's plan. I'm here to tell you this, **be different**. You cannot change the world by seeking their approval. Seek the approval of God.

This life is not a sprint, it is a marathon. You may have had a setback or a bad break, don't let that keep you down. Romans 12:2

says, "And do not be conformed to this world, but be transformed by the renewing of your mind, so that you may prove what the will of God is, that which is good and acceptable and perfect." God wants our lives to be transformed. We can be like the grandfather and try to please everyone around us or we can simply hear the voice of God.

Run your race. We are not racing against each other but we are fighting against, "spiritual *forces* of wickedness" (Ephesians 6:12). We have to point this world in the right direction. We are called to stand firm knowing who God is. God is cheering you on. He is there to support you when no one else will. We should always seek wise opinions and have humble heart, but at the end of the day don't get so distracted with what others say, that you forget to listen to what God has to say. **A world changer's journey begins when their own world has been changed.** We are called to renew our minds. It can be easy to seek behavior modification, but what we really need is heart transformation. We can only change this world one person at a time.

Run your race keeping your eyes on Christ. Francis Frangipane once said, **"People with faith were not just "believers"; they were world changers!"** Hebrews 11 has a list of men and women who used their faith to change their culture. Yet what caused them to do great things? There was something on the inside of them. They all had a spark that took place in their heart. They all had faith.

(29) YOU ARE CALLED BY NAME

The Apostle Paul once wrote "Or do you not know that the unrighteous will not inherit the kingdom of God? Do not be deceived; neither fornicators, nor idolaters, nor adulterers, nor effeminate, nor homosexuals, nor thieves, nor the covetous, nor drunkards, nor revilers, nor swindlers, will inherit the kingdom of God. **Such were some of you;** but you were washed, but you were sanctified, but you were justified in the name of the Lord Jesus Christ and in the Spirit of our God." (1 Corinthians 6:9-11).

Notice the words, **"Such were some of you."** Paul is saying that if you believe in Jesus, this is no longer your identity. I do not believe in living in denial, but I do believe that we need to see that this is what we were without Christ. God has now washed you of your sins and you should not associate yourself with these things.

As believers, we all struggle with sin. Some battle with lust others battle lying or what not. The Apostle Paul said his struggle was with coveting. We all face sin's temptation, but we must understand that **sin should never be the definition of who we are.** Don't attach yourself to titles such as: weak, defeated, sick, prideful, and much afraid. We must understand that because of the cross God has given us a new name.

Fun fact, while I was in High School, I joined the Worship Band *Called by Name* with Juan Martinez, Pops Cruz, and Trae Cruz. To me I've always remembered that phrase. When we worship, we need to keep in mind that God is calling our name. We in response need to call God by His name, He has many. He is our perfect father, wonderful counselor, mighty God, and Lord of all.

Mary Lea, a wonderful lady who goes to my Church gave a book for me to read called, "Hind's feet on High Places". In this book the author tells a story about young woman named Much Afraid (if you do not want the book to be spoiled I recommend you skip this paragraph). This story explains how Much Afraid who travels to the High Places in guidance by the Shepherd. As the book concludes the Shepherd gives her a new name, Grace and Glory. No longer will she be called Much Afraid but now she will be known as Grace and Glory. Throughout the journey she walked with sorrow and suffering, and later the shepherd changed their name to joy and peace. This speaks a message to me that God can use the suffering and sorrow that has been with us and turn it into something for our good.

Jesus once said, "...the sheep hear his voice, and he calls his own sheep by name and leads them out." (John 10:3). **It is important to know who you are, it is vital to know whose you are.**

Stop carrying the names that sin gave you and begin to walk in your new identity in Christ. We should remind ourselves of the names that God calls us. My friends **God is calling you by a new name today.** You are justified. You are sanctified. And you are called by name!

(30) YOU ARE SIGNIFICANT

One of the top questions ever asked is, "What is the purpose of my life?" When people feel unsuccessful in their life, they can feel hopeless and depressed. The truth is that Christ has a plan for your life. Many people want a single purpose for their life. The reality is that there are multiple reasons you have meaning today.

Now this is a broad question, and there is no one single answer for it. Every believer has a general and personal purpose for our life. Our personal purpose deals with the gifts and passions God has given to us. Our general purpose is to believe that Jesus died on the cross for our sins and preach the gospel. Around 1647, a group of Christians wrote a summary of beliefs about their faith. These were called the Westminster Catechisms. One of these writings was, "What is chief end of man? Man's chief end is to glorify God, and to enjoy him forever." I believe that this still rings true today.

So what do you have passion about? This is one way to find your personal purpose for your life. You can glorify God with your gifts and talents. I once heard someone say that, "God doesn't call the qualified, He qualifies the called." I don't necessarily believe that statement, so I'm here to bring a new perspective. Throughout the Bible God called the unqualified, the qualified, and anyone who would listen to His voice. He calls everyone! He calls you.

The Bible tells us that God, "...desires all men to be saved and to come to the knowledge of the truth." (1 Tim. 2:4). God's plan for your life is for you to be saved. He doesn't call a select few, He desires that, "all men" be saved. He is the answer. Remember there is not just one purpose for your life. We exist to believe in Jesus, use our passions for His glory, and to share this wonderful message of grace. You can have everything, yet still have a void on the inside. We can find significance in Jesus. Allow God to come into your life and fill the emptiness. Live life, glorify God, and enjoy Him forever.

(31) YOU ARE CAPABLE

Jesus once said, "I am the vine, you are the branches; he who abides in Me and I in him, he bears much fruit, for **apart from Me** you can do nothing." (John 15:5). Notice how we are connected to God. Because we are in Christ, we bear fruit.

Note also how this verse ends saying, "apart from me you can do nothing." Now there are many people who do not believe in Christ and do many great things. Some write great songs or produce funny movies. The point of this verse shows how in light of eternity, none of those things really mattered. What is the point if you, "gain the whole world but lose your own soul? (Matt. 16:26). We may be able to do great things through our own strengths, but that pales in compassion to what we can do through Christ.

So how do we bear more fruit? We do it through Christ. The Apostle Paul wrote, "I can do all things **through Him** who strengthens me." (Phil. 4:13). He is the one giving us life and fruit. There is a correlation from these two passages of scripture. One explains how we can do nothing apart from Christ, and the other tells us that we can do all things through Christ.

Without God we can do nothing of significance, but with God we can do all things. Who is the one that invigorates us? God, He is where our strength comes from. Did Peter walk on water through his own ability? No He walked because of Christ. It is when we keep our eyes on Jesus that we can do the impossible.

When we make it all about us, we will become discouraged. When we realize it is all about Him, we will be encouraged. Keep in mind where your strength is from. Tell yourself, "I can do all things through Christ who strengthens me."

(32) YOU ARE STRONG

The Apostle Paul once said, "Therefore I am well content with weaknesses, with insults, with distresses, with persecutions, with difficulties, for Christ's sake; for when I am weak, **then I am strong**." (2 Corinthians 12:10). He wrote this because of the great persecution he was facing. In spite of the great weakness that he felt, he was reminded that God was his strength, The Christian life is not Jesus plus my law keeping, obedience, and strength. No, it is Jesus plus nothing

Think about this, you cannot shoot an arrow unless the string of the bow is pulled back. Sometimes we feel pulled back, far away from where we want to be. Maybe it was a sickness, financial hurt, or a broken relationship. I'm writing you to tell you, even in our weakest moments when we feel stretched and pulled past our breaking point, God is working all things out for our good (Romans 8:28). **God can use what pulled you back to launch you into your destiny.** It's time to take two steps forward for every step back.

Be reminded that, "the joy of the Lord is your strength." (Nehemiah 8:10). True joy takes place when we rely on Jesus. There is something empowering knowing that God loves us. Don't leave any arrows in your quiver. Use them all. We all have been given tools for this life, utilize them for good.

Some of us try to throw our arrows. We try to do it all on our own strength. We launch it with every muscle we have. But if without the bow we can only go so far. Without Christ, we can only accomplish so much. In light of eternity, what can I accomplish on my own effort. But let me tell you that with Jesus, you can make an eternal impact into this world. You are significant! Your life matters and there is a reason that you are alive today.

How do muscles grow? According to *Built Lean,* "In order to produce muscle growth, you have to apply a load of stress greater than what your body or muscles had previously adapted too." When we have things pull us and hurt us, we can either let it keep us down or cause us to grow. God can take the ashes and make something beautiful. He can take the tension and stress that the enemy meant for your harm to make you stronger.

I love what God once told Joshua. Moses his leader, had passed away. He was now in charge of the nation of Israel. You can imagine the great worry and anxiety this can place on a man. God told Joshua, "This book of the law shall not depart from your mouth, but you shall meditate on it day and night, so that you may be careful to do according to all that is written in it; for then you will make your way prosperous, and then you will have success. Have I not commanded you? **Be strong and courageous!** Do not tremble or be dismayed, for the LORD your God is with you wherever you go."

(Joshua 1:8-9). What is the cure for trembling and fear? It is in knowing that we are not alone. It is knowing that God will be with us wherever we go. May you hear God telling you these same words, "Be strong and courageous!"

How can we go from a path of lack to the path of prosperity? We must meditate on God's word day and night. Then God will make our way prosperous. True supernatural strength can only come from God. Remind yourself of your identity in Jesus. Be encouraged that even when we feel weak or inadequate, **we are strong because of Jesus!**

(33) YOU ARE THE TEMPLE OF THE HOLY SPIRIT

When we study the book of 1 Corinthians, we discover that the Church in Corinth was going through some problems. They were a town with many ports. Thus, they had sailors from all around. Prostitutes began to become known and many in the church were committing immorality. Paul responds by writing this letter to remind them of their identity in Christ.

In the sixth chapter of this letter, Paul used the phrase, "Don't you know" four times. In this letter, we never hear Paul call them, "foolish" or "bewitched." Yet in Galatians when there was a confusion about (doctrinal issue) holding on to the law, Paul said this, "You foolish Galatians, who has bewitched you, before whose eyes Jesus Christ was publicly portrayed as crucified?"

There is something about knowing your identity in Christ that causes a man to get up when he has failed. The Scriptures tell us, "For a righteous man falls seven times, and rises again..." (Proverbs 24:16).

When the Apostle Paul heard there was sexual sin the church in Corinth, he told then, "... do you not know that **your body is a temple of the Holy Spirit** who is in you, whom you have from God, and that you are not your own?" (1 Corinthians 6:19). Paul's response to sin is to teach them about their identity in Christ.

When God first spoke audibly to Moses, he spoke through a burning bush. I love His attitude he says, "remove your sandals from your feet, for the place on which you are standing is holy ground." Even today when we enter a house, we take off our shoes as a sign of respect.

When you sin do you lose your righteousness? No, because you did not earn it from your deeds you cannot lose it because of your bad deeds. It was always, "by grace through faith." (Ephesians 2:8). Notice when this man falls he gets back up still righteous. It is in our moments of sin which we need to know we are righteous. Notice Paul never said their body "was" the temple; he said it "is" the temple of the Holy Spirit. Will this cause people to have a license to sin? Absolutely not, when we hear the true gospel of grace it causes our life to reflect our identity.

There is only one God, and He exists in three persons. There is the Father, the Son, and the Holy Spirit. Many of us know that Jesus loves us, but once in a while I encourage you to remind yourself that the Holy Spirit loves you.

Romans 15:30 tells us, "Now I urge you, brethren, by our Lord Jesus Christ and by **the love of the Spirit**, to strive together with me in your prayers to God for me,"

We may have a previous idea about what the Holy Spirit is like through people, but many times that is their reactions and it doesn't always give us a clear picture. Sometimes people may cry, get excited, fall out, or even laugh. Remember that the Holy Spirit is as sane, gentle, kind, humble, and loving as Christ was while He walked on this Earth.

What causes a church to turn from sin? It happens when they know who they are. **Many know that God loves them but how many realize that the Holy Spirit loves you too!** Take a moment from reading that and speak it out-loud, say, "The Holy Spirit loves me." Walk knowing that the presence of God is with you, and remember you are the temple of the Holy Spirit.

(34) YOU ARE COVERED IN GOLD

While Moses was leading the nation of Israel God told him, "Let them construct a sanctuary for Me, that I may dwell among them." (Exodus 25:8). What an amazing thought. As holy as God is, He wants to dwell with us. He wanted them to know that He was with them. God has now made us, "the temple of the Holy Spirit" (1 Corinthians 6:19). When we look to the temple of Moses we can see a visual representation of our identity in Jesus.

The tabernacle of Moses was made up of these beautiful standing boards. These were the walls of the temple. They got these wooden boards by cutting them down from Acacia trees. The Scriptures tell us, "For you will go out with joy And be led forth with peace; The mountains and the hills will break forth into shouts of joy before you, And all the trees of the field will clap their hands." (Isaiah 55:12). We are all like trees. These boards represent us as believers. When you got saved, God took you from the dry desert and made you a new creation (see 2 Corinthians 5:17)!

Now wood speaks of humanity, and gold speaks of the righteousness of God. After Jesus died on the cross, the temple curtain was torn from top to bottom. It was a sign that God was going to create a new temple. This time it was not going to be made up of physical gold but spiritual gold. The temple of God is now all of us as believers.

We are all standing boards. Each board is a picture of each believer. To make the walls of the temple they took the Acacia wood and covered them in gold. When you look at the temple, you don't see the wood, but instead you see the gold.

How can we be righteous before God? Because Jesus became sin on the cross. He took our sin and swapped it for His right standing with God. Now because of that beautiful exchange we are, "the righteousness of God in Him." (2 Corinthians 5:21).

When you look at other Christians, see them covered in gold!

When you look at other Christians, see them covered in gold as well! We may disagree here and there, but at the end of the day, they are just as righteous as we are. It's time that we see others the way God sees them.

The Apostle Paul wrote, "But we all, with unveiled face, beholding as in a mirror the glory of the Lord, are being transformed into the same image from glory to glory, just as from the Lord, the Spirit." (2 Corinthians 3:18). Now what does it mean to behold the glory of the Lord? Well the standing boards in Holy of Holies reflected the Ark of the Covenant. This was where God's shekinah glory would be.

Many times when writers in the Bible would describe the shekinah glory, they describe it as a cloud. Since these standing boards were golden, the glory of God's presence would shine like a mirror. Moses was speaking to the Lord and wanted God to go with him. Moses told God, "If Your Presence does not go *with us,* do not bring us up from here...Please, show me Your glory." (Exodus 33). God responded to him saying, "I will make all **My goodness pass before you**...You cannot see My face; for no man shall see Me, and live...So it shall be, while **My glory passes by**, that I will put you in the cleft of the rock, and will cover you with My hand while I pass by. [23] Then I will take away My hand, and you shall see My back; but My face shall not be seen." [5] The goodness and glory of God are synonymous. Do you want to see God's glory? See His goodness.

We are like those boards, we look to the cross and see the glory of the Lord. Because we are looking at the glory, we become like a golden mirror and reflect that same image.

Under the old covenant the physical temple was the place where God's presence dwelt. Today because of the cross, we are the temple of the Holy Spirit! Stand tall knowing you are covered in gold, and right before God!

---

[5] Lucas Miles actually shared the following story in one of his sermons.

(35) YOU ARE A CHILD OF GOD

There are so many great names of God. Some of these are, "El Shaddai, Elohim, Yahweh, and Yahweh Jireh." These names are all used to describe God. Did you know that when Jesus was on this earth He actually gave us a new name of God? This is one of God's greatest names, father.

The Bible says, "For you have not received a spirit of slavery leading to fear again, but you have received a spirit of adoption as sons by which we cry out, 'Abba! Father!'" (Romans 8:15). Jesus did a perfect work on the cross. **The moment you received God's free gift of salvation, you became a child of God.**

This word, "abba" is actually an Aramaic word people in Jesus' time would use. Some even translate this word as, "daddy" speaking of our closeness with God. If you were at a playground in Israel you would hear children calling out to go on the swing by saying, "Abba, abba." Imagine a young Hebrew child getting ready to jump off of the deep end of the pool. He wants his father to catch him, so he yells out, "Abba!" God wants us to have this child-like faith.

Just as a prince doesn't earn their spot in the kingdom, we don't either. A king doesn't choose the fastest or strongest child, they are born into their kingly family. In that same way we don't have to earn our relationship with God, it is a freely given. We can go boldly to God's throne not because of our works, but because He is our Father.

Psalms 68:5-6 tells us that God is, "A father of the fatherless and a judge for the widows, Is God in His holy habitation. God makes a home for the lonely; He leads out the prisoners into prosperity, Only the rebellious dwell in a parched land." One of the worst things that took place while writing this book was when my Dad passed away. There is just something about having a good Father in our life that makes us better. It's the way God designed it. Maybe your reading this book and don't have a great relationship your Dad. I want you to know that God is a perfect Father. The Prophet Isaiah speaks of some great names of God, "His name will be called Wonderful Counsellor, Mighty God, Eternal Father, Prince of Peace." (Isaiah 9:6-7). Remind yourself that God is your Eternal Father.

How do you see God? Do you see Him as an angry God? Or do you see Him as your loving father? How we see God impacts our relationship with Him. Jesus paid the ultimate price to have us born into the family of God. With so many great names of God, I believe that the simple name of, "Abba! Father!" is life changing (Rom. 8:15).

(36) YOU ARE SEATED IN HEAVENLY PLACES

The tabernacle of Moses is filled with beautiful furniture. It has the Lampstand, the Table of Showbread, and the Ark of the Covenant. Yet did you know that there are no seats in the tabernacle? Not one chair is mentioned. I believe this is a picture of how the work of the priest, under the old covenant, was continuous. Hebrews 10:11 says, "And every priest stands ministering daily and offering repeatedly the same sacrifices, which can never take away sins." Notice how the author of Hebrews describes how the priest is working, **he is standing.** This is because the sacrifices had to be made daily.

What was the first thing Jesus did when He got to Heaven after the cross? The Scriptures tell us, "**But this Man,** after He had offered one sacrifice for sins forever, **sat down at the right hand of God,** 14 For by one offering He has perfected forever those who are being sanctified." (Hebrews 10:12). The old covenant was something that took place repeatedly and daily, this new covenant is about a single act of love. Why did Jesus sit down? The work was finished. Jesus through one sacrifice has perfected us forever.

Ephesians 2:4-6 says, "But God, being rich in mercy, because of His great love with which He loved us, [5] even when we were dead in our transgressions, made us alive together with Christ (by grace you have been saved), [6] and raised us up with Him, and seated us with Him in the heavenly *places* in Christ Jesus," What does this mean to be seated in heavenly places?

Think about the growth of a baby. It does not begin by standing but sitting. It first learns to sit upright before it can walk. In the life of a believer we are called to do this also. We first sit down with Christ so that we will be able to stand and walk. Watchman Nee once said, "To sit down is simply to rest our whole weight—our load, ourselves, our future, everything—upon the Lord. We let him bear the responsibility and case to carry it ourselves." Fully place your trust in Jesus. Lean on His everlasting love.

God gave the Israelites a beautiful land full of milk and honey which was their Promised Land. As believers in Christ, our Promised Land is rest. Where are we today? We are already seated with Christ in Heavenly places. You may say, "But Caleb how can I be seated in heavenly places when I am here on this Earth?" This idea is to give you the knowledge that what happened to Jesus happened to you. When Christ died, we died also through Him. When He rose again, we were raised to life as well. And when it says that He sat down, so did we. Romans 6:4 echoes this truth by saying, "Therefore we have been buried with Him through baptism into death, so that as Christ was raised from the dead through the glory of the Father, so we too might walk in newness of life." We have been buried, raise to life, and seated with Christ! Can I get an amen?

Notice how the Scriptures tell us that He has seated us. This was not something we earned, but it was the work of God. Some people live their life trying to make it to Heaven without realizing that they are already seated in Heaven. Your seat is reserved, now is the time to do good works on this Earth today. Don't work to get to gain a better seat in Heaven; work because you are already seated.

This is done by our faith and His grace. When Jesus was on the Earth, a Mother came to Jesus to ask Him if her two sons could sit at Jesus' left and right side in Heaven. Jesus explained that they didn't fully understand what they were asking, and I believe that they were trying to earn their place with God. I wonder how big their eyes will be when they see everyone seated together next to Christ. The message of the gospel is not about earning your seat at the table. When we get saved, we are simply resting in what Christ has already accomplished.

(37) YOU ARE SEALED

Paul told the church in Ephesus, "In Him, you also, after listening to the message of truth, the gospel of your salvation-having also believed, **you were sealed in Him with the Holy Spirit** of promise," (Ephesians 1:13).

Before the days of Amazon Prime's two-day shipping and text updates from UPS, wax seals were an effective way to mail a letter. The wax seal gave identity because they knew who it was from. It gave security because what was inside was protected from being opened. Without it, you really didn't know if your letter had been tampered with. If you had been given a letter from your king which said, "The British the are on their way, send help!" how would know this was true? The seal was your way of knowing the true identity of the sender. In the same way, we have been sealed by the Holy Spirit and can know our identity and security in Jesus.

Do you ever feel insecure? Allow God to give you comfort and security today. Rest at night knowing you are forever secure in the arms of Jesus! This is why Isaiah 43:1 says that God, "...formed you...Do not fear, for I have redeemed you; I have called you by name; you are Mine!"

We don't have to wait for the Holy Spirit to show up. When you walk into church, the Holy Spirit goes with you. We are not just sealed by the Spirit, we are sealed, "with the Holy Spirit." He Himself is our seal. Jesus once told His disciples that the Holy Spirit will remain with us, **"forever;"** (John 14:16).

Who do we belong to? Since we are sealed with the Holy Spirit, we belong to Christ. The Scriptures tell us, *"and **he has identified us as his own** by placing the Holy Spirit in our hearts as the first installment that guarantees everything he has promised us"* (2 Corinthians 1:22) (NLT). We have just taken a glimpse into the greatness that God has in store for us. Later Paul also told the church in Corinth, **"you are a letter of Christ,** cared for by us, written not with ink but with the Spirit of the living God,"** (2 Corinthians 3:3).

Campus Crusade for Christ has a great illustration which shows us that Chocolate milk is a great way to think about the Holy Spirit. Picture this, we are the milk and the Holy Spirit is the choclate syrup. When we get saved, the Holy Spirit is placed in us. He is now with us, but notice that the choclate milk is still at the bottom of the glass. Sometimes we can't always see a changed life immediately after salvation. To be filled with the Spirit is a term used by Scripture to encourage us to stir up what is inside of us. When you stir up the glass, you get that beautiful tan choclate milk. My friend there is greatness inside of you. Just because you don't see it yet does not mean it's not there. Keep believing and stirring up the gift God gave you!

When the great flood took over the Earth, Noah and his family were sealed in the ark. Even though they may have tripped and fell, they would fall in the ark. Similarly, we are sealed with the Holy Spirit. Yes, we may fall and make mistakes, but when we fall, it's time to get back up and remember who we are in Christ.

Because you are in Christ, God has sealed you with the Holy Spirit. This seal gives us identity because God is saying, "you are mine!" (Isaiah 43:1). It also gives us a security of our salvation.

(38) YOU ARE MADE IN THE IMAGO DEI

Did you know that you are made in the image of God? When God first created Adam, He said, "Let Us make man in Our image, according to Our likeness;" (Genesis 1:26). You were created to mirror the likeness of Christ. He has set His imprint on the human soul. We are created in the *imago dei*. This phrase imago dei is Latin for the, "image of God." To say that we are the imago dei is to say that we are made in the image of God.

The Bible says, "But we all, with unveiled face, beholding as in a mirror the glory of the Lord, are being transformed into the same image from glory to glory, just as from the Lord, the Spirit." (2 Corinthians 3:18). This analogy of the mirror speaks that God wants us to look to Jesus. Just as we wake up and look in the mirror before we leave the house, God wants us to look to Jesus.

Anytime we sin and do not live a moral life, we are reflecting an image that is not of God. What He desires is that we live a life that represents our true identity. You are called to be an image bearer of Christ, proclaiming the gospel of Jesus through your actions, words, and life. We are called to reflect the peace, joy, patience, and love of God.

Many times, when we approach God, we look to ourselves, our insecurities, and our failures. Instead God wants us to behold, "the glory of the Lord." How do we behold Jesus? We behold Him by seeing Him in the Bible and listening to Christ-focused messages.

Every story of the Bible points to the cross. For instance, when you see the story of how Abraham gave up his son his only son, the son that he loved, you see Jesus. When you read about how Joseph was sold off for pieces of silver, we can remember how Judas sold Jesus for pieces of silver.

Under the old covenant, there was a huge veil about sixty foot high. This separated the people from God. Under this new covenant, we don't have any barriers between us and God. We are believers with an, "unveiled face." We can speak to God without fear. All of our sin has been punished at the cross.

Believe that God is a God of love. Never in the Bible does it say, "God is anger." Although we read of God's anger in the Old Testament, God is never defined as a God of wrath. Instead He is defined as a God of Love. The Bible explains that, "God is love" (1 John 4:8). Our life on this Earth is not a perfect example or image of Jesus. Yet still despite our flaws, God chooses us to be His hands and feet to this world.

It is the very fact that your sins have been removed that you can talk to God without a sense of guilt or shame. When we read the

Bible, we can see the love of God, and when we see the love of God, we are transformed into that same image. When we look to Jesus we see perfection, we see holiness, and we see love. People don't see the physical body of Jesus today. Instead the image they see is us, the body of church. We are called to be the hands and feet of God. When people see us they should be seeing the love and image of God!

(39) YOU ARE QUALIFIED

Chad Mansbridge wrote a really cool little book called, "He Qualifies Us" in which he says, "Under the Abrahamic Covenant; God's promises become your right and inheritance, because of your **Pedigree**. Under the Mosaic Law Covenant; God's promises are your right and inheritance, because of your **Performance**. But under the New Covenant Agreement, through the Gospel of Jesus; God's promised blessings are your right and inheritance purely because of your **Position**."

I think this is a great way to see these different covenants. Our identity in Christ is different from these covenants because it takes the focus off ourselves. So many times we try to find our identity through our performance and our pedigree. Yet in this new covenant it is about Christ's pedigree and Christ's performance. What is our part in this new covenant? Faith, our part is to believe in what Christ has done for us.

Paul told the church in Colossae, "[12] giving thanks to the Father, who **has qualified you** to share in the inheritance of the saints in light. [13] He has delivered us from the domain of darkness and transferred us to the kingdom of his beloved Son, [14] in whom we have redemption, the forgiveness of sins." (Colossians 1:11-14).

What was Paul writing to the church in Colossae? He was telling them to give thanks that God has qualified us to share in the inheritance. How did those under the Abrahamic Covenant receive their blessings? By their pedigree, they were blessed because of their family. Now we are in a new covenant where we are born again! We have been made sons and daughters of God. That is what it means to be born again and be born of the Spirit.

Nicodemus a prominent Pharisee came to Jesus in the night with some questions. As they talked Jesus explained saying, "I tell you the truth, no one can enter the kingdom of God unless he is born of water and the Spirit. Flesh gives birth to flesh, but the Spirit gives birth to spirit..." (John 3:3-7). Before we were saved, we were spiritually dead. Now that we have been saved, we have been made alive!

Too many times we subconsciously disqualify ourselves. We say things like, "I'm not eloquent enough. I'm not good enough. I'm not worthy." Yet continually through the Scriptures we discover that it is less about me and more about Christ. It is about Jesus' perfect pedigree and performance. Now because of the Cross we are qualified to receive God's blessings!

(40) YOU CAN DWELL IN THE SECRET PLACE

There are many ways to save a dollar. One way is to shop for things that are on sale. Every Black Friday we see many people trying to save money by buying things. Another way is by saving. Simply take the spare money you have and save it. Proverbs 13:11 says "…whoever gathers money little by little makes it grow." In the same way we all have **a memory bank.** The more we acknowledge the goodness of God, the more our faith will become productive. Paul told Philemon, "that the sharing of your faith may become effective **by the acknowledgment of every good thing** which is in you **in Christ Jesus.**" (Philemon 1:6) (NKJV). Live in daily thanksgiving towards God for saving, redeeming, forgiving, and loving us.

In Christ we have access to the father. Psalm 91:1 says, "He who dwells in the shelter of the Most High Will **abide** in the shadow of the Almighty." To be under a shadow is to be in a place of coolness and rest. Are you resting where God's shadow is? The, "secret place" is about abiding in Christ. It is a place of intimacy and closeness.

One of my favorite Pastors is Joseph Prince. In his book, *The Prayer of Protection*, he says, "When Psalm 91 talks about dwelling in the, 'secret place' of the Most High, that place is not a geographical location, but spiritual intimacy with our Lord Jesus."

The Hebrew word for, "dwell" is the Hebrew word, "yashab"(yä·shav') which means, "**to sit down, to remain, or to settle.**" Where are you camped at? It's time to pitch our tent in the presence of God. Are you living in a place of peace, or are you choosing to sit at the feet of Christ? The more you sit at the feet of Jesus and hear His words, the more your efficient your faith becomes. Remember, "...**faith *comes* by hearing,** and hearing by the word of God." (Romans 10:17).

Pastor Matt Chandler once said, "The greater your knowledge of the goodness and grace of God on your life, the more likely you are to praise Him in the storm." The secret place is not like a fisherman's favorite fishing spot, it is about knowing and have a close bond with Jesus. When Psalms 91:1 talks about the, "shadow of the almighty" it is speaking of God's defense. This word for shadow is the Hebrew word "tsel" which is same word used for protection appears in Numbers 14:9. This word means , "shadow, shade, and protection." If you are ever in a dry and sunny area, finding shade can very important; in some ways it could save your life. Are we guaranteed a life free from turmoil or tragedy? No we still live in a fallen world with fallen people.

There are wars, sicknesses, and hardships in this Earth. Yet in spite of this, we are called to be like David and pray for God's protection.

You get to decide how close you want to be with God. Dwelling in the presence of God does not mean we visit or vacation there; it is a constant state of closeness with God. It means that we, "Rejoice always, [17]pray without ceasing, [18]give thanks in all circumstances..." (1 Thessalonians5:16-18) (ESV).

How do we have useful, efficient, and effective faith? It is by the daily acknowledgement of what God has done for us. Take the anxiety, depression, and discontent out of your memory bank. Discover what you have been given in Christ. It's time to **take the promises of God to the bank!**

(41) YOU ARE A SAINT

Am I just a sinner saved by grace? Am I a saint? Or am I both? Semantics is the, "study of meaning." I believe that this question has become a bit of semantics. It all has to do with the definition of the word, sinner. If by sinner you mean, "someone who sins" then we are all sinners. On the other hand, if by sinner I mean, "we are born sinners" then only those who are non-believers fall into this category. Why? Because we have been made a new creation through the cross. Our old self has died and we are now born again and are now dead to sin. One of my hobbies is to play basketball, but I would not introduce myself as a basketball player. Why? Because that is not my identity. Yes, it is something I do from time to time, but it is not something I am defined by. Have I sinned, yes. Do I attach myself to the title of being a sinner? No.

The Bible says clearly, "¹⁹ For just as through the disobedi-ence of **the one man** (Adam) the many were made **sinners,** so also through the obedience of **the one man** (Jesus) the many will be made **righteous.**" (Romans 5:19) (brackets mine). When were we made sin-ners? When Adam sinned. By one man's sin, we were all made sinners. It doesn't matter if you never sinned in your life, you would still be a sinner. In man's definition of the word sinner is man's actions, but the Bible's definition of a sinner is by, "the one man's actions (Adam)". In the same way, we are not made righteous by our action, but we are made righteous by, "the one man's action (Jesus)".

Without Christ I am sinner unable to help myself, but with Christ I am a saint enabled to do the work of God! I'm not advocating that we ignore our sin, I'm advocating that we place our eyes on Christ. Paul wrote his letter to the church in Ephesus for, "...the [b]saints who are [c]at Ephesus..." (Ephesians 1:1). When he wrote to the church in Corinth he called them all saints. He said, "To the church...in Corinth, to those sanctified in Christ Jesus, called to be saints together with all those who in every place call upon the name of our Lord Jesus..." (1 Corinthians 1:2). **In the mind of Paul all believers are saints in the church.**

This word translated for, "saint" is the Greek word hagios. When you look at the first mention of this word in the new testament it is used to describe the Holy Spirit. This is found in Mathew 1:18 which says that Mary, "...was found with child of the **Holy (hagios) Ghost.**" He is the Spirit of the Saints. He is our holiness. When we call someone a saint, we are not saying their life is perfect but that they are holy because of Jesus. When you look across the aisle at church, see you're your fellow believers as saints. Treat them with respect and love because they are a set apart by God. Are you living your life by the labels sin has given you or by the names that God has given to you?

(42) YOU ARE CONNECTED

When we read the Bible, there are verses which may need commentary and explanation. In this chapter, I would like to look at a passage in John 15. Jesus once said, "If anyone does not abide in Me, he is thrown away as a branch and dries up; and they gather them, and cast them into the fire and they are burned" (John 15:6). Some people may become fearful reading this verse. We have to understand that this is for those who do not believe in Christ and people who are not a part of the true vine.

When I think of branches I immediately think about oak trees. At my Mom's house she has these huge pecan trees that are wonderful, and every so often a thunderstorm will come by and knock the branches off. In fact we have had to trim the branches many times because they would grow right next to the power lines. Power lines and trees do not get along. But this is not what Jesus was describing. He wasn't saying that next time you get go astray, God will cut you off. No the picture Jesus wanted to give you is that He is connected to us. Jesus is not the tree trunk and we are not the leaves. This was not the illustration given. Jesus said that He is the vine and we are the branches" (see John 15:1-3) We are one with Christ in the sense that we are connected to Him. He gives us that abundant life that we need.

What exactly does it mean to abide in Christ? If you believe in Christ as your savior, you are already abiding in the vine. Abiding in Christ does not mean that you have to work to keep your standing. This life is one that God supplies the ability. The reason I am able to love people is because of Christ. The reason I am able to bear good fruit is because of the Holy Spirit, who is inside me. *Got Questions.com*, a website filled with answers to questions of the Bible said, "**Therefore, abiding in Christ is not a special level of Christian experience, available only to a few; rather, it is the position of all true believers**[6]."

One of the most popular verses in the Bible says, "[13] I can do all things through Him who strengthens me." (Philippians 4:13). This is contrast to John 15 which says that, "Apart from Me, you can do nothing." What God wants to get us to understand is this reality is that you are not bearing fruit because of how great you are; you are bearing fruit because of who He is. It is that we are abiding in Christ that is why we produce good fruit. Abiding in Christ means that we believe in Jesus.

Jesus once said, "[20] For where two or three have gathered together in My name, I am there in their midst." (Matthew 18:20). Whether you are with a group of 300 people or 3 people, you can have church. Just remember there is a need for us to be surrounded

---

[6] "What does it mean to abide in Christ? Got Questions Ministries, n.d. Web. 17 Mar. 2015. <http://www.gotquestions.org/abide-in-Christ.html>.

by other believers. One of the best parts about being a Christian is that you are a part of a family. Don't neglect the gathering together of believers. We have brothers and sisters in Christ who are connected to us through Jesus. God has given us one another so that we can help each other.

Not every tragedy that happens to your life is God's will. Sometimes we are vines who get hit with the storms and wind of this world. It tries to destroy us, but thankfully **we are connected to a source of life.**

(43) YOU ARE LIFTED UP

Psalms 3:3 tells us, "But you, LORD, are a shield around me, my glory, the One who lifts my head high." (NIV). God wants you to keep your head lifted high. When we go through a tough patch God is saying, "Chin up! I am with you." I can imagine David writing this thinking about how God was a shield around him. What an amazing picture of God, He is a, "shield around me." May we constantly remind ourselves of how God is around us.

GotQuestions.org tells us, "What a divine trio of mercies is contained in this verse! -- defense for the defenseless, glory for the despised, and joy for the comfortless." John 15:1-3 tells us, "I am the true vine, and My Father is the vinedresser. ² Every branch in Me that does not bear fruit, **He takes away (airó)**; and every *branch* that bears fruit, He prunes it so that it may bear more fruit. ³ You are already clean because of the word which I have spoken to you."

The word used for, "he takes away" is the greek word, "airó." This word literally means, "To lift up." When you are not bearing fruit, God lifts you up! Remember when Jesus healed the paralytic man and told him, "Get up, **pick up (airó)** your bed and go home." (Matthew 9:6). He was using this word airó to tell the man to lift up his mat. Jesus was not saying to cut the bed. Is this what airó meant in this situation? No, Jesus wanted him to keep his mat and bring it home as a testimony.

Paul Ellis the author of *The Gospel in Ten Words* wrote, "Unfruitful branches are lifted out of the dirt and re-dressed so they can be nourished by the sun. Sticking with that metaphor, the reason why some Christians are barren is that they're facedown in the dirt and not looking at the Son."

What is interesting about vines is how they do not really have branches; they are literally all vine. Jesus is the vine and we are in Him. God wants you to bear fruit. I want you to bear fruit. If I want an oak tree to bear fruit, I continue to water it. The last thing I would do is cut the tree down. Then I would have no fruit and no tree. If God wants you to bear fruit he will continue to lift you up from the dirt of this world. When vines grow to the ground they become dirty and cannot bear fruit. They will get stepped on and ruined. The best thing to do is to lift the vine up. This is what God does, He lifts you up. He cleans you, "because of the word" (John 15:3). He brings the best out of you. God is described in Psalms 3:3 as, "...**the One who lifts my head high**." (NIV).

(44) YOU ARE CHOSEN

Winston S. Churchill once said, "A pessimist sees the difficulty in every opportunity; an optimist sees the opportunity in every difficulty." In the story of Esther, we can see how God used a young orphan girl to become the Queen of Persia for a perfect time. All Esther had was her voice and she was able to use it.

The story of Esther takes place during the Jewish exile. They had been defeated by Babylon and taken as slaves. Later the Persians defeated the Babylonians and the Jews found themselves under King Xerxes. A man named Haman had wrote a degree to annihilate all of the Jewish people in their nation. The King had signed the decree not realizing that his Queen Esther was a Jew as well. When Esther finds this out she risks her life and appears to see the king in the inner court without being summoned. The law that they were under said that she should have been killed unless the king held out his scepter towards her. She used her bravery and was not killed, she later told the King about this and this moment was used to save her people!

She was a Queen, "for such a time as this" (Esther 4:14). My friend there are going to be moments when you are going to be needed to stand up for righteousness. God has plans for your life to accomplish and fulfill many visions. Esther could have looked at herself and said, "Who am I to be used by God? I am only an orphan in a foreign land." Yet God used what she had (her five loaves and two fish) and saved her whole nation!

Abraham Lincoln once said, **"I will prepare and someday my chance will come."** Be ready, the Lord is looking for people who are ready to be used by God. Get into a local church, serve your community, and stay connected with people who love God.

Yes, we may not all have that big Esther moment when we push open the doors, risk our lives, and speak to a king. But I'm writing this to tell you that there are going to be moments in your life when you are able to make a difference. Be like Esther and see the opportunity in the difficult times. One of my friends Sam Cunningham once said, "The book of Esther is really about people serving God in difficult times." In this life, we will go through adversity. God wants us to remember that He is with us. He has good things for us. **God want us to be the light that this world needs.** The name for Esther is, "Star." It is appropriate because that's what she was. It was very dark for the Jews during this time. Yet God used Esther to be a light!

What is your gift? Sometimes you can discover your gift through a process of elimination. You can also look at this world and see what the needs are. Can you fulfill a need? Then use that ability to fix it. Sometimes God wants you to sow a seed. Other times God wants you to water a seed. And other times God lets us reap a seed.

Eugene Peterson gives a great paraphrase of 1 Timothy 4:12-14: "And that special gift of ministry you were given when the leaders of the church laid hands on you and prayed—keep that dusted off and in use" (The Message Bible). I love the thought of dusting off and using the gifts which we have. We all have different gift and abilities. You don't have to be the funniest comedian to make someone laugh, the best landscaper to mow someone's grass, or the richest businessman to buy someone's meal. You have been chosen by God to reach the people around you with the love of Christ!

(45) YOU MATTER

G. K. Chesterton once said, "All men matter. You matter. I matter. It's the hardest thing in theology to believe." Out of all the things in life we must understand, the love of God needs to be at the top. That is really what we are called to do. Jesus at the young age of twelve was found sitting in the temple asking questions. Before you start your day tomorrow, begin to ask quality questions.

The very first question in the Old Testament is, "Where are you?" Genesis 3:8-11 tells us, "They heard the sound of the Lord God walking in the garden in the [c]cool of the day, and the man and his wife hid themselves from the presence of the Lord God among the trees of the garden. ⁹ Then the Lord God called to the man, and said to him, 'Where are you?'" In the midst of their sin, God went to them. He is not going to abandon you. When we make a mistake, the Lord is there with grace. God was asking a question that we should all ask today, where am I? Today ask yourself, "Where am I going? These questions will help us to grow in grace and wisdom.

The very first question in the New Testament was, "Where is He?" Matthew 2:1-2 says, "Now after Jesus was born in Bethlehem of Judea in the days of Herod the king, behold, wise men from the East came to Jerusalem, ² saying, 'Where is He who has been born King of the Jews? For we have seen His star in the East and have come to worship Him.'" Why did the wise men go to see Jesus? They just wanted to worship Jesus. C. S. Lewis once said, **"Look for Christ and you will find Him. And with Him, everything else."** Why do we go to church today? When we go to church to worship Jesus, we are like the wise men.

When John the Baptist heard that Jesus wanted to be baptized by him, he was in shock. The New Living Translation describes the interaction by saying, "But John tried to talk him out of it. 'I am the one who needs to be baptized by you,' he said, 'so why are you coming to me?'" (Matthew 3:14). Also when Peter saw Jesus getting out the bucket of water and towel to wash his disciples feet, he was stunned. Peter wanted to wash Jesus' feet. Perhaps when John saw his cousin Jesus, he felt that he didn't matter enough to baptize Jesus. Maybe Peter didn't feel that he mattered enough to have his feet washed. I think Jesus was telling John and Peter, "What you have been doing is great, you matter to me." Ask the right questions. Maybe you are wondering, "Do I matter?" I want to echo the words of G. K. Chesterson, you matter to God!

(46) YOU ARE CALLED TO BE AN AL-PHA

Revelation 21:4-6 tells us, "…Then He who sat on the throne said, "Behold, I make all things new." And He said to me, "Write, for these words are true and faithful." And He said to me, "It is done! **I am the Alpha and the Omega**, the Beginning and the End. I will give of the fountain of the water of life freely to him who thirsts."

God offers salvation to anyone who desires it. The book of Revelation is a book full of symbols. It is also controversial so there are many interpretations on this book. I love the first verse which says, **"The Revelation of Jesus Christ**, which God gave Him to show His servants—things which must shortly take place. And He sent and signified it by His angel to His servant John," (Revelation 1:1). Whatever you believe about Revelation, you should have a revelation of Jesus by the end of it.

Think about relationships, why does God want men to be the head of the house? Because it is masculine energy to lead. This is the way God ordained it. Men are not to be egotistical and rule in a damaging way, but we are called to love as Christ loved the church.

Imagine a couple hiking, the man leads in front to make sure there isn't any danger on the road ahead. Also, the man should be the last. A true man places himself before others. If the ship is going down, the man should be the last one onto the rescue boat.

We are all called to love just as Jesus loves. Let's be alpha's and be the first one give, serve, help, and love. Do you ever see Jesus trying to prove who He was? No, instead we see Him leading because He knew that He was the alpha and the omega. **Many of us men want to be the alpha male, but are we willing to be the omega as well?** Are we willing to be a servant to our friends, family, and the people we love? Because that is the true heart of a great leader.

When we think about our identity, it also important to keep ourselves healthy. If we are setting a good example and spreading the gospel, God is going to want us to live longer. We cannot invite anyone to church in Heaven. If you live for fifty years, you have fifty years to advance the Kingdom of God. Obesity and lack of a good diet is something that hurts the gospel. When we workout and eat right, we are pleasing God. If we die, let it be from persecution or old age, not from an unhealthy lifestyle. Being an alpha means that we take care of the body God has given to us.

In Revelation 21:6 God identifies himself as the "Alpha and Omega." Alpha is the first letter of the Greek alphabet, and omega is the last letter of the alphabet. In other words, God is the "beginning and the end." The Hebrew language uses, Aleph-Tav, **for the first and the last. Jesus is the aleph-tav.** Does this mean that this was the authors intended meaning, no but Jesus is throughout the old testament. In many Scriptures, this Aleph-Tav is left untranslated. I believe that we can look at this and remember that Jesus is there even when we don't realize it. God was there in the beginning and He will be there with you until the end!

If you do not believe in Jesus, you will face a second death, but if you have faith in the Cross, you will not perish! Our life will not come to an end because He gives us, "eternal life" (John 3:16). Jesus is the, "...**author and finisher of our faith...**" **(Hebrews 12:1-2)**. The one who gave us the strength to begin this marathon of faith will be there at the end. Let Jesus lead your life because He is the true alpha!

(47) YOU ARE HOLY

There was once a group of blind men who touched an elephant to learn what it was. One man touches the leg and concludes, "Elephants are like trees." "Oh no," says the man gripping the ear. "Elephants are like huge fans." "You're both wrong," says the man feeling the tail. "Elephants are like snakes." I believe this is the picture many of us have when we try to describe the word, "holy." We may have a part of what it is but not the whole picture.

One of the main reasons we don't understand this meaning is because we put the emphasis on the outward rather than the inward. **Holiness is not what you wear, what you drive, or how long you pray. It is a work of grace.** According to the *New Unger's Bible Dictionary* holiness is from the Saxon word, "halig" which means, "'whole, 'sound[7].'" God has placed us in Christ where we are complete. There is a void inside all of us that only God can fill. The word holiness also means, "'separation,' or 'setting apart[8].'" We are in this world but not of this world.

---

[7] Unger, Merrill F., R. K. Harrison, Howard Frederic Vos, and Cyril J. Barber. *The New Unger's Bible Dictionary*. Chicago: Moody, 1988. Print.
[8] Ibid

Holiness is the combination of a couple things. I believe that **holiness is being set apart while whole and complete.** God is set apart from sin while being absolutely complete. The Bible proclaims, "And by that will, we have been made holy through the sacrifice of the body of Jesus Christ once for all." (Hebrews 10:10) (NIV). Never look to your behavior to see how holy you are. Instead look to Jesus and see how holy you are. He has cleansed us of all of our sins. Every time you take communion remind yourself that because Jesus' was body was broken, **you are whole in Christ!**

The blind men could not describe the elephant piece by piece, they needed someone with open eyes to give them the whole picture. In the same way, we need God to open our eyes to our new identity in Christ. Because of the cross, He has set us apart from this world and made us complete. Now we can rejoice that He has made us holy!

(48) YOU ARE FAVORED

God never intended for man to suffer. His plan, in the beginning, was for life. Yet, by one man's sin, "death reigned." The word used in Romans 5:17 (the verse we read in the second chapter) for, "reign" is the Greek word, "*basileuō.*" According to Strong's Lexicon, this word means, "to be king, to exercise kingly power, to reign." It is quite clear that death ruled the earth because of Adam's sin. Yet, when we look to the Cross we can see a bright future. Just as death reigns because of Adam's sin, we can reign in life through Christ. How do we do this? By doing two things. We are called to receive an **abundance of grace** and the **gift of righteousness**. When we tap into these two conductors, we will begin to see our lives radically change.

What is grace? To me, it is not just a belief system or a doctrine, it is so much more. It is the gospel. Christ is grace personified. He is the picture of what it means to reign in life. Grace is unmerited favor. When the Apostle Paul talks about the gospel, He mentions how it is the gospel of grace and peace. God blesses us not because we deserve it but because Christ deserves it.

Nothing is free in this world, so how can God bless us freely? He causes us to have favor on our lives **because of the Cross.** Too many times when we pray to God, we try to think of reasons why we deserve it. Yet it is not about earning, it is about receiving. Jesus once said, "For I say to you that unless your righteousness surpasses that of the scribes and Pharisees, you will not enter the kingdom of heaven." (Mathew 5:20). When Jesus said these words I can imagine the hustle and bustle of the town. People in the Marketplace. Kids moving around. The wind blowing through the trees. I'm sure Jesus didn't always get the chance to speak with a completely silent group. Yet when Jesus says they have to be better than the Scribes

Christ is Grace personified

and Pharisees, I'm sure the town went silent. The ears of everyone were in shock. How can this be? Remember the Pharisees were focused on works and deserved favor. These were the best of the best. The only person whose righteousness surpassed the scribes and Pharisees was Jesus.

We are called to receive Christ's righteousness. This is what grace is all about. Grace is God's unmerited favor. This not only applies to Salvation but to almost every area of our Christian life. It is time to take in an abundance of grace!

(49) YOU ARE ANOINTED

Psalms 23 goes down as one of the most popular chapters in the Bible. I believe that there is a hidden emerald in this passage which I would like to share with you. Remember Psalms 23 is explaining how the Lord is our shepherd, we are His sheep, and He is leading us. Jesus once referred to Himself as, "the good shepherd" (John 10:11). Psalm 23:5 tells us, "⁵ You prepare a table before me in the presence of my enemies; You have anointed my head with oil; My cup overflows." Did you know that oil was used in the ancient shepherding community? They would take the oil and work it into their face and ears to help protect them from insects and ticks. We understand how God protects us from the big wolves, but He also wants us to be protected from the small bugs in this life.

The Scriptures tell us, "Catch for us the foxes, the little foxes that ruin the vineyards, our vineyards that are in bloom." (Song of Solomon 2:15) (NIV). Sometimes it's the small foxes that we allow to ruin our day. Ask yourself, "Is it worth worrying about?" Let's make sure that we major on the major things and minor on the minor things. The Scriptures tell us, "⁷ You have loved righteousness and hated wickedness; Therefore God, Your God, has anointed You

With the oil of joy above Your fellows." (Psalms 45:7). Oil is also described in the King James Bible as the, "the oil of gladness" (Psalms 45:7). Notice how oil of joy causes the flies of depression, anxiety, and fear to leave. God has anointed you, don't let what others say about you effect you. People's negative words can be like flies. We have to get that oil of gladness and stay full of joy! Anointing Oil is always poured on the person's head and it drips down. God does not want you living stressed out. He wants you to have joy.

Three types of people were anointed in the old testament prophets, priests, and kings. Only specific people were anointed under the old testament. Yet in this new covenant the anointing is for everyone who believes. Paul told the church in Corinth, "²¹ Now **He** who **establishes us** with you in Christ **and anointed us is God**,"(2 Corinthians 1:21). What was reserved for a narrow and select group of people is given now given freely to all who believe!

In Exodus 30:30 God said, "You shall anoint Aaron and his sons, and consecrate them, that they may minister as priests to Me." Notice how the priest were anointed and consecrated. This word for consecrated is the Hebrew word, "*gadash*" which means, "to be set apart, dedicate, prepare, sanctify." Under the old covenant only a select group were priests, the Levites. Now because of the Cross, God has made the church a "royal priesthood" (1 Peter 2:9). Gifts and talents have nothing in comparison to the anointing of God.

(50) YOU ARE GOD'S TREASURED POSSESSION

In the 1980's a father dropped his son off at the Elementary School. It seemed to be a typical day in this small town of Arminia. As he was a mile away, a devastating earthquake ripped through the streets. Immediately an estimated 25,000 people were killed. This father rushed to his son's school only to find that the school had been flattened. There was no sign of life.

Though his prospects appeared hopeless, the father began feverishly removing rubble from where he believed his son's classroom had been. Courageously, he worked alone; no one volunteered to help him. With strength and endurance beyond himself, **he began to dig** and dig, and dig…for 8 hours…12…24…36 hours.

Some told the father to go home, that there was no chance that any of the pupils could be alive. To which he always replied, "I made my son a promise that I'd be there for him anytime he needed me. I must continue to dig."

Then in the 38th hour, as he heaved away a heavy piece of rubble, he heard voices. "Armand!" he screamed. A child's voice responded: "Dad! It's me…Armand!" Moments later, the dad helped his son and 13 students climb out of the debris When the building collapsed, these children had been spared in a tent-like pocket. How amazing!.[9]

This is a human story about a human father. How much more does our Father God care for us? Jesus once said, "If you then, being evil, know how to give good gifts to your children, how much more will your Father who is in heaven give what is good to those who ask Him!" (Matthew 7:11)

God once told the nation of Israel, "Now therefore, if you will indeed obey my voice and keep my covenant, you shall be **my treasured possession** among all peoples, for all the earth is mine;" (Exodus 19:5) (ESV). Under the old covenant you had to obey to be God's treasured possession, and I believe that under grace it is a free gift that God gives.

How you see God effects how you hear Him. My friend just as that father began to dig through the debris for his treasure (his son) how much does God care for you? Jesus gave His life for us. He endured the cross, "for the joy set before Him" (Hebrews 12:2). Who is the joy described in this verse? **You are His joy.** You are God's treasured possession!

---

[9] Complete footnote **https://www.crossway.org/tracts/a-fathers-love-2770/**

(51) YOU SMELL GOOD

One day while Jesus was visiting someone's house, a lady named Mary Magdalene brought Jesus an alabaster jar worth a year's wages. Her tears ran down her face as she broke the jar and poured on Him. She did this to prepare Jesus, "for burial" (Matthew 26:12). Jesus told her, "Your sins are forgiven" (Luke 7:48). When Mary had poured that alabaster jar, **the aroma would have filled the room** and would have had clothing that was saturated with that aroma. When you spend time next to a campfire, the smoke moves toward you, that aroma goes with you. When you do positive actions, you are changing the atmosphere. Some people cause the room to smell by their attitude, but when you step up and do something positive, you are have a sweet aroma.

How can we smell? By the oxygen in our lungs. God created us by breathing. He, "formed man of dust from the ground, and breathed into his nostrils the breath of life; and man became a living being" (Genesis 2:7). The absence of God is the absence of life. If we do not have faith in Christ, we will "perish" (John 3:16). Crucifixion on a cross was not just death by the nails, but it is death by suffocation. The cross was a gruesome death because the victim had to lift themselves up in order to breathe. Typically, if the Romans wanted to complete the execution of a criminal, they would break their legs so they could not pick themselves up. This is why it was so rare that Christ was pierced in the side. One of His final words on the cross was, "It is Finished." He gave His spirit to God and breathed His last. Jesus gave His last breath for you so that you and I can have eternal life,

Why does Isaiah talk about how even righteousness can be like a filthy rag? Image I was going to make you breakfast. I get out a plate from the locked china cabinet. I place fresh cooked stack of homemade waffles, bacon on the side, and a hot cup of caramel coffee. After that I go outside and take a spoonful of dirt and sprinkle it on top. Would you eat it? No, that's because while waffles are a great breakfast, it is dirt that makes it filthy. In the same way our righteous acts are not filthy rags by themselves, they are filthy because of sin.

When we sin, our robe gets stained. Righteous acts alone are not filthy rags to God, it is the contamination of our sin that causes even our best clothes to have an oder of sin, Without Christ our righteousness is like "filthy rags" (Isaiah 64:6) (NKJV).

Is that who we are today? Are we unclean, filthy, or dirty? Is that our current identity? The Scriptures tell us, "For we are to God **the sweet aroma of Christ** among those who are being saved and those who are perishing." (2 Corinthians 2:15) (Berean Bible) What is your identity today? You are a sweet smell aroma to God. 1 John 1:7 tells us that the blood of Jesus, "cleanses us from all sin." This word is describing what takes place at this moment. God wore our sin stained robe on the cross and gave us His robe of righteousness.

(52) YOU ARE UNIQUE

When I was around the age of eight, I can remember realization that I couldn't snap my fingers or whistle. I was distraught. My brother Josh and I tried to figure out the technique, but nothing happened. He was able to whistle, but not me. It was like the clouds followed me, the flowers turned away from me, and as I looked up I cried out, "Everyone can whistle except me!" As an adult you realize how silly it is. Even if I can't snap, I have other things that matter more than that. This is how some feel about talent. They believe that only the people who preach, sing, or play an instrument can make a difference in the church. This is just not the case.

Paul once wrote, "For just as we have many members in one body and all the members do not have the same function....Since we have gifts that differ according to the grace given to us, each of us is to exercise them accordingly..." (Romans 12:4-6). There are many parts in the body of Christ and we all have a role.

The first man in the Bible with the Spirit of God was Bezalel. He was no musician, preacher, or deacon. He was a construction worker. He was appointed to build the tabernacle of God and the treasured Ark of the Covenant. There was a young Pastor who was intimidated because he did not have a loud boisterous voice. This was the beginning of his ministry. He doesn't talk like Morgan Freeman. But still he found out that using the voice that God gave him was what worked best. He said, "In my early days as pastor…I felt as though my laid-back personality was a disadvantage… But

INSTEAD OF LOOKING AT WHAT YOU CAN'T DO, LOOK AT WHAT YOU CAN DO

what I thought would be a liability turned out to be an asset. I realized that God made me like this on purpose." (Every Day a Friday P.98-99)[10]. This man is Joel Osteen, he Pastor's one of the largest Churches today. He realized that he did not have to talk loudly, instead he just had to move the microphone closer. He used the voice God gave him. My word to you is this, use what God gave you.

Maybe you can't sing, snap, or whistle, but instead of looking at what you can't do, look at what you can do. Can we pay for someone's meal? Can we hug a sad friend? Can we pray for the sick? When we embrace the gifts that God gave us, we will impact this world.

---

[10] Osteen, Joel. *Every Day a Friday: How to Be Happier 7 Days a Week.* New York, NY: FaithWords, 2011. Print.

(53) YOU ARE MORE THAN A CON-QUEROR

Romans 8:35-37 tells us, "Who shall separate us from the love of Christ? Shall tribulation, or distress, or persecution, or famine, or nakedness, or peril, or sword? As it is written: "For Your sake we are killed all day long; We are accounted as sheep for the slaughter." Yet in all these things **we are more than conquerors through Him** who loved us." (NKJV). This word loved is in the past tense, it means that before we were even born, God loved you. Long ago, God set His heart on you. This is not a picture of you barely crossing the finish line, running out of breath, about to fall over. No, this a picture of you at the end of barefoot marathon, booking it in a full sprint!

The King James Version says, "I'm persuaded". Paul was saying, in essence, that he was convinced. The case for grace was one he believed in. If I could paraphrase the words of Paul, "Destroy my body and I'll be with Christ. Let me live, and I'll be Christ to those around me."

So, what does it mean to be more than a conqueror? How can this be? Because it was never our battle. Let's repeat the same words as Jahaziel when a large army was about to attack the Israelites,

"...the battle is not yours, but God's. (2 Chronicles 20:15). **The battle is the Lord's!** Because Christ conquered death, we are also conquerors. Death has been conquered. Pastor Greg Laurie once said, "Death died when Christ rose." When Jesus was raised from the dead on that bright Sunday morning, death was defeated.

Tim Tebow once said, **"What God knows about us is more important than what others think."** What Jesus did on the cross not only effects our future, it effects this very moment. I encourage you to continue and read the entire chapter eight of Romans, it will help you understand your true identity. It is by far one of the best chapters in the Bible. Leonard Ravenhill once said, "Romans 7 is the funeral march. Romans 8 is the wedding march." Nothing can separate you from the love of Christ. Even during times of persecution, Paul was reminded that God's love had not changed.

On the cross what happened to Him, happened to us. He was crucified, buried, raised, and seated in heavenly places. So are we today; we have been buried, raised, and seated. Not only are you loved, you are more than loved. Not only are you forgiven, you are more than forgiven. I think everyone knows that they've been given grace, but we do not fully understand the magnitude of God's grace. Not only are we conquerors because Christ conquered sin and death, we are more than conquerors!

(54) YOU ARE IN CHRIST

Thich Nhat Hanh once said, "**Love in such a way that the person you love feels free**." When I think about this quote. I see the way Jesus loves. We all are given a choice to have eternal life or eternal death. You are free in Christ. I believe this can be used in many areas of our life such as our evangelism and relationships.

Jesus once told His disciples, "whoever does not receive you, nor heed your words, as you go out of that house or that city, shake the dust off your feet." (Matthew 10:14). We are called to tell people about the good news of Jesus, but if they do not receive it, we are not supposed to force our belief on them. We must dust our feet off and keep moving forward. Leave the door open for more discussion, but do not let it discourage you.

Jesus also once used a parable to explain how we share the gospel. He said, "The sower sows the word." (Mark 4:14). Some of the seeds are placed on the ground but are later snatched up. Others went on "the rocky places who, when they hear the word, immediately receive it with joy" but have no root (Mark 4:16-17). Finally those who are good soil, receive it and bring back a, "thirty, sixty, and a hundredfold" return (Mark 4:20). What is our calling as fellow believers? We are called to continue and sow the word.

We can grow through the help of others. Some people give us water and help us grow. Others shine light on our soul and help us even more. Each part plays a role the planting, the watering, and the sunlight all help in the growth of the plant. I don't know if this is just my personal experience, but every time I hear someone talk about self-help books, they always bash them. Ultimately you are reading a book that was not written by yourself. So, it is not your ideas. It's really other people helping you. In a similar way, this is what the Apostle Paul was doing except His writings were inspired by God. It's just a title that helps everyone know what genre your book is. To seclude ourselves away from the advice of God and others is no help to ourselves.

What does it mean to be in Christ? On the cross what happened to Him, happened to us. He was crucified, buried, raised, and seated in heavenly places. So are we today; we have been buried, raised, and seated. Remember, "For freedom Christ has set us free; stand firm therefore, and do not submit again to a yoke of slavery." (Galatians 5:1). It is knowing the love of God that causes us to live a moral life. Loving with freedom allows evangelism and our relationships to be fruitful. May we continue to love in such a way that those around us feel free.

(55) YOU ARE BELOVED

The story of David and Goliath has to rank as one of the most famous stories in the Bible. It resonates with us because of the consistent message. God does not look at the outward, but he looks at the heart.

The passage of Scripture which talks about this battle discusses how the Israelites and Philistines were at a standstill. Both armies on each side. One man from each army was to go and fight, the victor wins the entire battle. For forty days' no one would face Goliath. He was over nine-foot-tall and wore very heavy armor. Yet here arrives David, a young shepherd's boy who was probably around the age of 15-16 years of age. He decides to fight Goliath, but not with a sword or shield but, "…in the name of the Lord…" (1 Samuel 17:45). As David goes toward Goliath, he strikes the giant with a sling and a stone. Goliath falls face forward, and David takes his own sword to decapitate him.

There is significance in the names of David and Goliath. The name Goliath in Hebrew means, "Exile." He is from Gath which means, "Winepress." Many times, in the Bible winepress represents God's judgement (Isaiah 63:2; Lamentations 1:15; Revelation 14:20). Revelation 14:19 tells us, "So the angel swung his sickle....and threw them into the great winepress of the wrath of God." When we put the two together, he is Goliath (exile) from Gath (winepress/God's judgment). Satan has been exiled because of God's judgment and he wants you to believe that you too are exiled from God.

David's name in Hebrew means, "beloved." What does it take to kill a Goliath? No tanks, bazooka's, swords or daggers, it takes someone who knows they are loved by God. Many people live in defeat because they think they are under God's wrath because of what they have done wrong and what they haven't done right. What we have to understand is that God has paid for our sins. All we have to do is receive what he has done.

We are no longer an exile from God because of wrath. The punishment, judgment, and condemnation we deserved was placed on Jesus. Now we have right standing with God through Christ payment. Some have this idea that Jesus is the one full of love but God has anger. The truth is that they both have a heart of love. In fact, John 3:16 tells us, "For God so loved the world..."

David was wearing shepherds clothing and King Saul wanted him to wear a soldier's armor. It didn't matter what he was wearing. He knew his identity! It takes someone who knows they are beloved by God to conquer giants.

CLOSING THOUGHTS

Throughout this 55 chapter book we have seen the many ways God has given grace to us. I would like to show you one final way to get grace. It is found in I Peter **5:5** which says, "Likewise you younger people, submit yourselves to your elders. Yes, all of you be submissive to one another, and be clothed with humility, for 'God resists the proud, But **gives grace to the humble**'" (NKJV). It takes humility to know that we cannot earn, deserve or merit God's favor.

The goal of this book is to magnify the Gospel. The greatest prize that we have is to know Jesus. Wisdom is described as a women. "Long life is in her right hand; In her left hand are riches and honor." (Proverbs 3:16). God doesn't want us to just go after the hands of wisdom, He want us to embrace the person of wisdom. We are called to give wisdom a hug. When you hug someone their arms wrap around you. When seek the Lord all these other needs will work out. Today Jesus is our "wisdom" (1 Corinthians 1:30). **Go after Jesus with all that you have.**

The Bible informs us that, "For as he thinks within himself, so he is." (Proverbs 23:7). What you do is wrapped up in how you think. In a world that goes up and down, we need something stable in our lives. How do you see yourself? It is time to see ourselves as God sees us. Do you see yourself as accepted? Ephesians 1:6 tells us we are, "accepted in the Beloved." Christ is described as the beloved and we are accepted in Christ. Do you see yourself as loved? Romans

8:31-39 explains that nothing can separate us from the love of God. Do you see yourself as forgiven? Colossians 2:13 declares that, "He forgave us all of our sins."

We are the body of Christ. The more we know Christ, the more we know our purpose in life. If a Christian says, "Look at me, I pray twenty-five hours a day. I'm holy in and of myself" they're prideful because no one is perfect. Also, if someone says, "I am a lowly sinner, woe is me." they have swung the pendulum too far the other way. Our behavior should not define our identity, instead our identity should effect our behavior. The truth is that without Christ I am nothing, but with Christ I can do all things!

God changed Abram's (High Father) name to Abraham (Father of many), Sarai's name to Sarah, Jacob's name to Israel, Simon's (Reed) name to Peter (Rock), and used Jacob to change his son's name from Ben-oni (Son of my sorrow) to Benjamin (son of my right hand). God is doing the same thing today! He is changing your name from: depressed to peaceful, broken to healed, anxious to hopeful, and from sinner to a saint!

David longed for a pure heart; we have one today in Christ. Job wished that he had a mediator; Jesus is our mediator today. Moses signed and wanted the whole nation to be priests, today we are! We truly don't realize all of blessings in this new covenant. **We are really twice as blessed** than we realize. We get more grace by knowing Jesus, resting in His finished work, and by humbly receiving it through faith.

ACKNOWLEDGEMENTS

Erica Robles, my love, I'm thankful for her spirit! Many times, as I was working on this book, she would bring me some fresh China Chef (the best restaurant in Bay City, Texas) and a Dr. Pepper. Every time I see her, she lights up and I see God's joy in her eyes!

Can't forget about my Mom, Shelley Gibson, thank you! From a young age you believed in me. I think that's how God is. He doesn't just see where we are, He sees where we can be. That's why you're a great Mom because you always believe for a greater tomorrow! Thank you to my Dad, Captain Harold Gibson! He was always project minded. May we all have his attitude towards a good book. When he read a book he enjoyed, Dad would give it to everyone.

Thank you, Joshua Gibson, my big brother! He has always been a great support. He is always well organized and every book needs that. When I first began writing papers in College, he was there to help guide me! Also, thank you to my sweet sister Hannah Gibson! I always prayed to not be the youngest child and I'm so glad God answered that prayer! She has a great Instagram page called @Grace.Upon.Grace_ made for Godly encouragement.

Larry Martinez and Jamey Escamilla, I am blessed to be their friend. Many days I would call up Larry and ask him questions about the Bible. He is really full of wisdom. They inspire me!

My Meadors family, this book will be difficult to read because it's never quiet in a room full of Meadors. Thank you: Peggy, Lyndon Bryan, Angie, Canon, Angela, Joseph, Ella, Jack, Jake, Victoria, Kali, Nathan, Mario, Sheilah, Rick, Lindsay, Bri, Makayla, Craig, Nolan, Cameron, Owen, Ian, Russell, Kim, Brandon, Janice, Ralph Sr., Ralph Jr., Somer, Cydney, Kobe, Avorie, Tanner, Dana, Dave, Dustin, Kassidy, Austin, and Mylee.

Shoutout to the Robles crew for all your joy and great music: Efrain Sr., Adela, Ronald, Adriana, Esme, Isaiah, Israel, Efrain Jr., Julia, Raymond, Ada, Analisa, Ari, and Romeo.

Thank you to the Preachers whose Church I was a part of. Pastors: Bobby and Michelle Williams, Jim and Sharon Hardaway, Chester and Peggy Sassmon, Sonny and Rosie Salas. Youth Pastors: Abel and Leisha Hurtado, Renee and Ricky Chavez, Luke and Mary Grace Kunefke. Missionaries: Don and Sarah Reed. All of them showed me what grace looks like in everyday life!

High Five Church, I appreciate ya'll so much! Thank you: Scotty, Mary Lea, Gilbert (Brother G), Debbie, Juju. James Sr., Nick, Rebecca, Michael (Coach), Luddy, Michael Jacob, Jonathan, Christina, Henry, Chrystal, Malcom, Layla, Lyzah, Marcus, Santa, Bob, Becky, Eric, Jenna, Katie, Levi, Alaina, Buddy, Patricia, Damon, Lacey, Phoebe, Payton, Penelope, Mason, LeNae, Martin, Marty, Abilene, Kirstie, James Jr., James, Nancy, Fabian, Rosalinda, Mike, Pam, Jordan, Miss Sandy, Penny, Sean, every person who has ever walked through those doors, and Bobbbyyy!!

Thanks to Colleen Vavra (Colleen's Camera Clicks) for her heart for God and the free photo shoot for this books profile photo! I also want to thank my H-E-B crew: Roosevelt, Maria-Christina, Zulema, Ernest, Andrew, Steven, and all of my 292 family! Also props those who helped me edit this book: Mom, Larry Martinez, and Chris Barhorst, also Writeralways16, and Roxanam84 from Fiverr! Thank you Mike Reddell for allowing me to write a column each week in the Bay City Sentinel (local newspaper company).

Pastor Lucas Miles thank you for you work and guidance in my life. God has given you a voice, I'm thankful you are using it! Shout out to our awesome grace group of Pastor's from around the United States that Lucas and Mark Machen put together: Al Jennings, Chris Barhorst, Clint Byars, Dennis and Denise Capra, Jordan Orick, and Kevin Casey! To the many other teachers who broke the brick wall to let others walk through it: Joseph Prince, Rob and Ryan Rufus, Andrew Wommack and Paul Ellis.

BIBLIOGRAPHY

Rhymer, David. 2005. Between text & sermon: Jeremiah 31:31-34. *Interpretation* 59, no. 3: 294-296, http://search.proquest.com/docview/202695848?accountid=44880.

Maier, C. M. (2008). Jeremiah as teacher of torah. *Interpretation, 62*(1), 22-32,4. Retrieved from http://search.proquest.com/docview/202697668?accountid=44880

Morschauser, Scott. "GOOD FIGS, BAD FIGS: JUDICIAL DIFFERENTIATION IN THE BOOK OF JEREMIAH." *Hebrew Studies* 50 (2009): 406-8, http://search.proquest.com/docview/216677285?accountid=44880.

Moberly, R. W. L. 2012. Knowing god and knowing about god: Martin buber's two types of faith revisited; the midianite-kenite hypothesis revisited and the origins of judah; the midianite-kenite hypothesis revisited and the origins of judah. *Scottish Journal of Theology* 65, no. 4: 402-420, http://search.proquest.com/docview/1142095710?accountid=44880.

Terry, Justyn. 2013. The forgiveness of sins and the work of christ: A case for substitutionary atonement. *Anglican Theological Review* 95, no. 1: 9-24, http://search.proquest.com/docview/1284118629?accountid=44880.

Kaiser, Walter C, Jr. 1972. "The old promise and the New Covenant : Jeremiah 31:31-34." *Journal Of The Evangelical Theological Society* 15, no. 1: 11-23. *ATLA Religion Database with ATLASerials*, EBSCO*host* (accessed June 29, 2014).

Photos used in this book are from Shutterstock.

FREE RESOURCES

To read more of Caleb's articles check out,

CourageWithGrace.org

If you are ever in Bay City, Texas, make sure to check out High Five Church. This world is always trying to bring us down, so at High Five we are here to encourage and lift you up! Make sure to check out our church at **highfivechurch.com**

Thank you for reading this book! If you have an Amazon account, I would really appreciate an honest review! **An Amazon review is the #1 thing you can do to help this book get to more people!** I want to know your thoughts!

Made in the USA
Las Vegas, NV
22 February 2022

44345230R00090